Happily Ever After

Happily Ever After

Folktales that Illuminate Marriage and Commitment

MELISS BUNCE

August House Publishers, Inc.
LITTLE ROCK

Published 2003 by August House Publishers, Inc.
P.O. Box 3223, Little Rock, Arkansas, 72203,
501–372–5450.
http://www.augusthouse.com

Printed in the United States of America

10   9   8   7   6   5   4   3   2   1

LIBRARY OF CONGRESS CATALOGING-IN-PUBLICATION DATA
Bunce, Meliss, 1951–
Happily ever after : folktales that illuminate marriage and commitment / Meliss Bunce.
p.   cm.
Includes bibliographical references.
ISBN 0–87483–674–3
1. Marriage—Folklore. 2. Interpersonal relations—Folklore. 3. Tales. I. Title.
GR465.B85 2003
398.27—dc 21   2002043797

Executive editor: Liz Parkhurst
Project editors: Cindy Michaels, Pam Strickland
Cover design: Patrick McKelvey, AdMan, Inc.
Interior design: Liz Lester Design

The paper used in this publication meets the minimum requirements of the
American National Standard for Information Sciences—Permanence of
Paper for Printed Library Materials, ANSI Z39.48–1984.

AUGUST HOUSE   PUBLISHERS   LITTLE ROCK

To my beloved husband,
Tom Casciero

ACKNOWLEDGMENTS

It gives me enormous pleasure to thank all of the fine people who have helped me create this book.

First of all, I am grateful to J.J. Reneaux, who was a terrific storyteller and a lovely woman. It was J.J. who first named this work as my calling. My heartfelt thanks go to Donald and Merle Davis, cherished mentors and friends. I especially appreciate Merle's support for my presentation at the National Storytelling Conference, which became the genesis of this book.

Many of my colleagues in the storytelling community offered story suggestions. Others gave me tremendous assistance and encouragement. I am grateful to Gail Rosen, Alice McGill, Carolyn Rapp, Robin Moore, and Beth Vaughan. I am also grateful to Seska Ramberg, Marita Oosthuizen, Ladan Nabet and her uncle Hassan Momenzadeh, Carol Van Gorp, and the excellent staff of the Enoch Pratt Free Library for their assistance. A big thanks to Annie Hawkins for encouraging me to write and for providing much wise counsel.

Scholars in the folklore and theatre communities were incredibly generous in answering my questions and verifying sources. I'd like to thank Hasan El-Shamy, Esiaba Irobi, Margaret Read MacDonald, Moira Smith, Mary Beth Stein, Peggy Yocum, and Jack Zipes.

Deep appreciation goes to my editor, Liz Parkhurst; her unwavering enthusiasm for the project and her gracious support made this a delightful adventure.

Special thanks go to the four couples Tom and I have shared so much with—Carol and Gene Currotto, Carol and Rene DeLisle, Michael and Kate Gaudreau, and Paris Kern and Eric Winzenberg. The long-standing successes of their relationships fed my faith that "happily ever after" is possible.

A most special thank-you to my dear, wonderful daughter, Larken Bunce. Her perspective, wisdom, and keen eye helped tremendously in my writing. And my heart overflows with gratitude to my husband, Tom Casciero, for his enthusiastic, unending support of my storytelling and writing endeavors. He patiently read this book word for word, and his observations and suggestions enriched it immeasurably.

CONTENTS

Introduction   xi

THE HUNDRED YEAR FRIENDSHIP: STORIES OF SUCCESS

What He Loved Best of All   3
WALES

The Weaver King, the Warrior Queen   9
ARMENIA

Wealth, Wisdom, Women   15
EASTERN EUROPE

One Hundred Coins   21
FUJIAN, CHINA

The Linden and the Oak   27
GREECE

BAD LUCK AND BIG TROUBLE: CAUTIONARY TALES

When Peter Churned the Butter   35
NORWAY

Reflections on a Marriage   41
JAPAN

A Cake for Sholom and Sarah   49
POLAND

The Selkie Wife   55
SCOTLAND

Who Should Close the Door?   61
INDIA

The Wife Who Would Not Be Pleased   67
FINLAND

THE HOPE CHEST: STORIES OF COMFORT AND GUIDANCE

The Love Potion   73
KOREA

The Sweetest Thing in the World   81
CZECHOSLOVAKIA

Who Knows What Could Happen?   87
IRAQ

Strawberries   91
CHEROKEE, NORTH AMERICA

Keep Your Wife Well Fed   95
SWAHILI, KENYA

Saint Peter's Blessings   101
CUBA

What Women Most Desire   107
ENGLAND

APPENDICES

Epilogue   117

Some Thoughts for Storytellers on Using this Book   121

Sources for the Stories   127

Additional Resources   141

INTRODUCTION

When I was a little girl, I loved the fairy tales and folktales that ended "and they lived happily ever after." I took those stories deeply into my heart and believed them, every word. It seemed to me that phrase was a promise, my birthright: when I grew up, I *would* meet a handsome prince and we *would* fall in love and naturally, we *would* live happily ever after.

When I was eighteen years old, I entered a relationship that lasted twelve years. Life with a partner was a rude awakening for me, for no one had taught me how to be part of a couple. My parents had made a pact that they would never fight or even disagree in front of their children. To my young eyes, my grandparents, my aunts and uncles, and my parents' friends all seemed equally agreeable.

Movies and television in the 1950s and 1960s were of no help; the only couples who ever quarreled were *The Honeymooners* and since I always heard the adults laughing at them, I didn't think they were supposed to be taken seriously. This was decades before Family Life or Family Studies courses were offered in high school or college. There were also those "mystery romances" and "historical romances" and all of the other novels that always ended with the hero and heroine together, forever, happily. It was not a childhood that would foster a realistic approach to a relationship.

Now, I could point to a number of factors that spelled failure for my first long-term relationship. But I honestly think that the primary cause of our breakup was simply this: neither one of us had had any initiation into the inner workings of a marriage. No one ever took me aside and said, "This is what you must do to make a relationship work." The nuts and bolts, the foundation stones, the underpinnings of partnership were invisible to me. Left to my own devices, I was what Charlotte Mayerson calls a "sleepwalker." In her book *Goin' to the Chapel,* she discusses how two types of young women—"sleepwalkers" and "calculators"—think about marriage. Sleepwalkers like me more or less daydreamed their way into marriage, "under the spell of unexamined girlhood romance."*

---

* Charlotte Mayerson, *Goin' to the Chapel: Dreams of Love, Realities of Marriage* (New York: Basic Books, 1996).

Later, when I met Tom and considered making a serious commitment with a man for the second time, I had become more of a "calculator." Mayerson writes that "calculators make specific connections between marriage choices and the life they want for themselves."* I had my own previous experience to draw from, as well as a more mature view of the couples around me. As an adult, I saw plenty of folks living together who didn't get along very well. It was very disheartening, especially for someone whose favorite stories still ended with "and they lived happily ever after."

But I was determined to succeed with Tom. So, for the past fifteen years, my quest as a partner and wife has been to answer the question: "How can we live happily ever after?" I've spent a lot of time and money on courses, seminars, and therapy. I've read a ton of books and listened to a lot of other people's stories about their triumphs and disasters. I've created and collected stories about couples and crafted performances about marriage, commitment, and family. And I keep learning, trying every day to be a better partner, to understand my husband and myself a little more.

I wish I'd read stories like the ones in this book when I was growing up. I wish I had prepared myself more adequately for marriage. Though I am a happy, satisfied wife now, I regret the grief and turmoil of my first, unsuccessful relationship.

I wrote this book because I believe that, as an artist, I have an obligation to my community. For better or worse, we are all products of the culture we live in, and artists contribute substantially to every aspect of that culture. The stories we hear and read and watch and live are a sizable part of our heritage. *Happily Ever After: Folktales that Illuminate Marriage and Commitment* is my contribution to changing our perceptions about intimate partnerships. It is the first collection of folktales devoted solely to the celebration of the loving union possible for two dedicated hearts. In a world that has come to believe that "happily ever after" is only a fairy tale's ending, these stories offer the fresh, enlivening models of partnership and marriage that we all deserve.

After selecting these folktales from the vast number available, I researched their cultures and traditions and then carefully, respectfully retold them in my own words.

---

* Charlotte Mayerson, *Goin' to the Chapel: Dreams of Love, Realities of Marriage* (New York: Basic Books, 1996).

I've included humorous, poignant, provocative tales from around the world. In the first section, the successful relationship is not the focus of the stories; rather, it is a significant tool that helps the couples resolve their problems. The second section features cautionary tales that serve as warnings of the sorts of behavior that can wreak havoc in a relationship. In the final section, the characters in the stories struggle with the same frustrations and misunderstandings that befall every couple at one time or another. Their discoveries and reconciliations are welcome reassurance that loving harmony is possible.

Not so very long ago, folktales served people like you and me as their principal source of moral education, history, therapy, spiritual training, and entertainment. People would *use* stories in their day-to-day lives, telling and listening to them over and over again from childhood through old age. The images and messages were treasured for their inspiration, guidance, and collective wisdom.

These folktales are priceless gifts from the world's couples, crafted by people just like you, to help you prosper in your relationship. They work best if you allow them to become part of your daily lives. Read them, talk about them, read them again, argue about them, tell them to your friends, read them out loud to each other in bed, ruminate on them while you're walking or driving somewhere. If you have faith in the power of Story, they can serve you as they have served generations of couples before.

May you live Happily Ever After.

the Hundred Year Friendship

Stories of Success

What He Loved Best of All

WALES

Willy was a good lad, for all he was so slow. He was gentle with the lambs and there wasn't a dog for miles around that didn't wag its tail when Willy came by. He could coax a tune from a reed whistle and he knew where the violets first came up in spring. But all his brains wouldn't fill up a sparrow's egg, and that grieved his poor mother sorely. "Who will look after you, son, when I'm dead? You can't take care of yourself, your head's as empty as a beggar's purse. Ah me, what's to become of you?"

Willy found a sunny spot sitting in front of the house to ponder this question as best he could. Thinking was hard work for a fool.

Meg was the neighbor girl, lived down the road aways, and she liked Willy, fool or no. She could count up to twenty on her fingers and toes and she churned butter by the pound. She could weave a basket snug enough to fetch water and she had seven silver coins saved up in a stocking under her pillow. Meg came by with a pot of broth for Willy's mother and saw the young man scowling and scratching his head.

"What's the matter, Willy?"

He told her what his mother had said.

"Well now, there's old Annie, lives down in the hollow, and she knows everything in the world, most likely. Maybe she would know how to fill up your empty head." She took the pot inside the house.

Willy went tripping over his own feet, galloping down the road to the old woman's cottage, and he banged on the door. Annie was stirring something in a big kettle over the fire. She cocked an eyebrow and looked him up and down.

"What do you want, Willy?"

"Ma'am, I want something to fill up my head, ma'am. Ma says it's empty as a beggar's purse, and Meg said you would know how to fill it."

"That Meg is a smart girl. But what should go into a head, Willy? Feathers?"

Willy thought on that one. "Maybe . . ." He told her that the farmer called him a feather-head sometimes, but he decided he wanted something heavier than feathers.

"Heavier. Hmm. Mush, maybe?" Willy didn't see her sly smile.

Willy frowned and thought as hard as he could. "Maybe . . ." He told her the tinker called him a mush-head whenever he came by. "Is mush heavier than feathers, ma'am?"

"A bit heavier, Willy. How much do you reckon you'd need?"

Willy looked around her house and picked up a pottle from the table.

"My, my. Two helpings. And what would you do with mush in that head of yours?"

Willy dug his toe into the dirt floor for a long time and then he asked her if mush would make him smart, like his ma.

"No, boy, not mush. Brains. Brains is what makes you smart. If it's brains you wanted, why didn't you say so?"

Old Annie told Willy that he could get some brains if he would bring her the heart of the thing he loved best of all.

Willy screwed up his face and asked her what that would be.

She chuckled and shook her head. "Well now, *that* would be for you to figure out. I'm done with you, Willy. Take this for your mother and get back home." She gave Willy a small jar that she filled from the pot and closed the door behind him.

It took Willy most of the week to settle on the thing he loved best. It was bacon—crisp, juicy, sweet bacon. Why, he could eat a flitch of it! My, wasn't he pleased with himself for thinking of that!

When he told his mother what he was going to do, she smiled faintly. She was unhappy at losing the pig, but if old Annie said the pig's heart would help her son get brains, then she was agreeable to it. So Willy killed the pig and cut out the heart, wrapped it in a cloth, and traipsed back down to old Annie's. She was out in her garden, cutting long stems of ghosty-grey leaves.

Annie shook her head when she saw the bloody mess he'd brought. "Tell me, lad, what runs but has no feet?"

Willy stood with his mouth open, his lower lip quivering. He didn't know.

"Try again, Willy. That didn't get you any brains."

So Willy turned around and trudged home discouraged. When he got up to his cottage, there were crowds of people inside. Seems that while Willy was visiting old Annie, his mother had died. He sat down beside her and took her hand and cried and wailed and blubbered till the neighbors couldn't bear the noise of it and left him alone. Meg, the neighbor girl, stayed a while, patting his shoulder and giving him rags to blow his nose.

The next morning Willy sat down before the cold, empty hearth, his arms hanging between his knees, staring at the ashes. He remembered his mother till his heart was sore. She had been good to him, always kept him fed and warm, mended his clothes, and taught him his manners. Along about midday, it came to him that he loved his mother best of all. Better than Christmas cakes, better than kittens, even better than bacon! And for the first time that day, he felt happy, knowing what he should do.

It took him a while, but he finally found a sack big enough. He stuffed his mother's body into it and dragged it down the road to the cottage in the hollow. Old Annie was sitting before the fire, petting her ginger cat.

She peered into the sack and then looked at the young man sternly. "Tell me, Willy, what has a mouth but no eyes?"

Willy squinted at the ceiling and fidgeted for awhile. He didn't know.

Old Annie patted Willy's arm. "Try again, son. That didn't get you any brains."

Willy headed home, tears splashing in the dust as he walked. Halfway there, he sank down on the side of the road and bawled. After a bit, Meg came along.

"What's the matter, Willy?"

He told her everything, how he had taken old Annie the pig's heart and then his mother's body. He said nothing worked and now his mother was dead and he didn't have any brains and there was no one to look after him in the whole wide world.

"Well now, Willy, I could look after you. We could get married. What do you say to that?"

He sniffed and gulped and chewed on his cheek a while. Then he asked her if she could make tansy pudding and patch trousers and tell him when to take his cap off indoors.

Meg laughed. "I sure can. And lots more, too."

So that satisfied Willy. They got married, and the both of them were happy. Willy did the plowing and sowing and threshing. He herded the sheep and cut wood for the fire. Meg cooked and sewed and tended the chickens. She did the spinning and weaving and banked the fire every night so it never went out.

Willy played the whistle and Meg sang along. He showed her where to find wild mushrooms and she showed him how to wind yarn on a spindle. And at night, well, even a fool knows what to do when a woman hugs him close and whispers in his ear.

Time went by, and one day Willy was sitting out in the sun when a thought came to him, like a fly lighting on his nose. So he went to the garden and told Meg that since she was so kind to him and never yelled at him for being foolish and baked the tastiest apple tarts, he reckoned he loved her best of all.

Meg grinned at that and gave Willy a kiss. "I'm real glad you figured that out, Willy. Takes some folks a whole lot longer to know who they love the best, and they're not even fools."

He frowned and asked her in a worried voice if that meant he should take out her heart and go see old Annie about his brains. Meg patted his arm and told him no, he could take her with him just the way she was, with her heart still inside.

So they walked together down the road to the hollow, and there was old Annie, staking her hollyhock flowers beside the cottage door.

"What do you want, Willy?"

He told her that he had brought the heart of what he loved best and he was hoping to have his brains, now, please. She looked at the two of them and nodded. "So tell me, Willy, what's red and round on the outside and white with a star on the inside?"

Willy gave it his best, then he shook his head and sighed. He didn't know. Meg tugged at his sleeve and he bent over for her to whisper in his ear. Willy nodded eagerly.

"An *apple*, ma'am. It's an apple! You know, when you cut one crossways over the middle, the seeds make a little star in the very heart of it. And I know that's true, 'cause Meg here told me."

Old Annie smiled. "I told you Meg was a smart girl, Willy. Looks to me like you've got your brains!"

The young fellow stared at her blankly for a moment then looked all around him. Finally he turned to Meg and she whispered to him again. Then Willy straightened up with a grin that cracked his face from side to side.

"Yes ma'am, thank you, ma'am, I surely do!"

Old Annie stood at her doorstep and watched the two of them walk off down the road, holding hands. The old woman called out after them. "Hey Willy! That Meg of yours? She's a *lucky* girl, too!"

One of the greatest joys of my marriage is our friendship. There's nothing more comforting than knowing that Tom really, truly believes in me and will support me in whatever I do. I have kept faith in and nurtured him over the years as well. We've always been the other's biggest fan and cheerleader, encouraging one another whenever one of us wavered or wearied. Thoreau describes our friendship beautifully: "They are kind to each other's hopes, they cherish each other's dreams."

Our friendship is especially meaningful to me because he likes me even when I am a noodlehead. Someday you may come to the startling realization that your partner is a bit of a fool. If you are very wise, you will realize that you still love her or him anyway. The sooner you understand this, the sooner you can begin practicing tolerance, compassion, forbearance, and kindness—all the qualities that you naturally employ when dealing with someone who's doing the best they possibly can with what they have, one who is a child of the universe.

Take care of one another and be grateful, always, for the one who is foolish enough—and wise enough—to love you.

The Weaver King, the Warrior Queen

ARMENIA

O nce there was and there was not the son of a king. Prince Vatchagan was a skilled and fearless hunter. He roamed the mountains in search of bear, chased deer across the plains, and stalked lions in the valleys. When the young prince was twenty, the king and queen urged him to choose a bride. Vatchagan promised that he would seek a wife soon, but in truth he thought no more of women, for he far preferred hunting.

One day he traveled deep into a rugged valley. After a morning's hard riding, Prince Vatchagan drew up at a stream near a small village. There, as he knelt to drink, a young woman appeared.

"Here, stranger, you may drink from my jug." The prince looked up and nodded but could not speak, for she was the most beautiful woman he had ever seen. She was slender as a willow, with dark hair caught up in a thick braid and lips red as a ripe pomegranate. The woman filled her jug with clear water but she did not give it to Vatchagan. Rather, she poured it out onto the ground at his feet. Again she filled the jar—and again she emptied it. Twice more she filled and emptied the jug before she held it out to him. "Here, stranger, you may drink safely now."

Water had never tasted so sweet. When the young hunter returned her jug, she smiled. "Our water is very cold, from the snow off the mountain. I did not want it to harm you after your long ride. Shall we let your horse drink now?"

The two sat beside the stream and talked while Vatchagan's horse grazed. Her name was Anait and she was the only child of her old father, Aran the shepherd. He had taught her to ride at his side, herding their longhaired sheep and goats. When wolves preyed on their flocks, she had learned to defend them with spear and bow and arrows. Vatchagan was impressed by her common sense, strength, and courage. He told Anait only that he was a hunter, no more; he wished to be valued for himself, not for his royal blood. Vatchagan thought that she would not guess he was a prince, dressed in his simple huntsman's breeches.

Vatchagan and Anait went to her father's hut where Aran greeted them. Woven rugs covered the walls and floor, rugs more beautiful than the most prized carpets in the royal palace. Anait served them a tray of fruit, then sat down at her loom. The young prince watched in amazement as her nimble fingers flew, knotting woolen strands of sage green and cinnabar, poppy red and dusky blue into graceful, intricate patterns.

When Vatchagan asked the old shepherd for his consent to marry his daughter, Aran gazed long at his only child. It was clear that she was willing to marry the handsome stranger, but the old man was not so quickly persuaded. He asked the young man if he had a craft or trade.

When Vatchagan admitted that he did not, Aran spoke gravely. "Do you not know that fate can tumble even the greatest to the dust? I will not have my daughter hungry and in rags. Come back when you have mastered a craft and can support her."

The prince opened his mouth to protest, ready to explain that a trade was not necessary for someone who would soon inherit a throne. But he heeded the old man's words and kept silent. Humbly, he bowed his head before Anait's father.

"I will return when I can prove myself worthy of your daughter's hand, Old Father." Then he looked up into Anait's keen grey eyes. "Till that time, remember that I burn with love for you, Anait."

Her smile lightened his heart, but her words stunned him speechless once again. "I will wait for you, Prince Vatchagan," she whispered. Vatchagan rode home slowly, savoring each moment of his meeting with Anait. It was clear to him that she was more than a poor shepherd's daughter, and he was determined to wed her.

The prince wasted no time. Days once spent on horseback he now passed before a loom, as the best weavers in the kingdom taught him their art. When the king and queen suggested marriage to a neighboring princess, he refused, vowing he would marry one woman and one only. They assumed that he would soon lose interest in mastering such an exacting craft, but Vatchagan was steadfast; the memory of Anait's beauty and her far-seeing mind kept his heart enflamed.

After three years, Vatchagan galloped back into the valley and sought his beloved. In her father's hut he spread out a rug, woven of brightly dyed wool and thread of spun gold. The rug was filled with the colors Vatchagan knew—lapis, topaz, amethyst, ruby, the hues of the flowers and birds in the palace gardens.

Aran was impressed. "This is a fine gift, my friend, but have you learned a craft?"

Vatchagan replied with pride. *"This* is my trade, Old Father. I have become a weaver like your daughter. Now will you consent to our marriage?"

The entire village was invited to the wedding at the royal palace. Never was there a lovelier bride or a happier groom. The feasting lasted seven days and seven nights, and the dancing went on till the strings and pipes could play no more.

In the fullness of time, the old king and queen died and Vatchagan and Anait ascended to the throne. He taught Anait to read the words in books, while Anait taught him to read the hearts of men. Together they listened to those who petitioned the king, noting who was sincere and who wished to deceive. Every night, before they retired, the two would stand on a balcony overlooking the fast-flowing river that ran through their great land from one end to the other. As the evening star sparkled over-head, Anait would listen to the water whispering to itself.

Then one night, Queen Anait heard the voice of the river change. It muttered and grumbled, grating at its banks. She warned King Vatchagan that all was not as it appeared in their country. "I will care for the kingdom in your stead, but you must go out hunting again. There is something dangerous in the land and you must find it."

The king disguised himself as before and roamed his country, looking and lis-tening as Anait had taught him to do. At first all seemed well and the young king wondered if his wife was mistaken. But then he came to a city at the foot of a great mountain where he heard rumors that people were disappearing without a trace. In the marketplace he spied a tall, lean man with gold bands jangling about his arms and ankles, singing in a shrill, quivering voice. Vatchagan watched as people got up from their stalls or left their children or dropped food from their hands to follow the singer as he went weaving through the crowds. One glimpse into that man's narrow, glittering eyes and the young king knew that this stranger was something more than he appeared to be, something dangerous. He joined the others as the man moved slowly out of the gates of the city and led them up the mountain.

They reached a lonely pass just as darkness closed in. Suddenly armed bandits surrounded the dazed crowd, and before their eyes the charming singer changed into a giant serpent with cold, sinister eyes and golden rings circling his body. His henchmen pushed a boulder out of the rock wall, and the Serpent Demon herded his stunned captives into a huge, shadowy cavern deep in the mountain. The strong and fit were put into chains to be sold as slaves. The old and feeble begged for mercy, but the evil serpent devoured them.

When Vatchagan was pushed forward, he looked into his captor's eyes without flinching and declared that the serpent could profit more from his skill as a weaver of rugs than from his price as a slave. The greedy demon reluctantly agreed to spare Vatchagan, hissing threats of death if he did not prove his worth promptly. When the others were led off the next morning to join a caravan of slaves, the king was chained to a loom and given the brightly dyed wool and thread of spun gold that he asked for.

Days and weeks passed. Vatchagan did not return, nor did he send any word to his queen. When Anait stood on the balcony each evening, the river rushed by, booming and rolling with foreboding. Meanwhile, King Vatchagan sat at his loom and feverishly wove a rug glowing with rich colors and lively patterns; it was plain for all to see that this was a rug of unsurpassed beauty. The words that Vatchagan had woven into the rug were there in plain sight for all to see as well, but only those few who could read would recognize the strange golden markings for what they were. When it was finished, Vatchagan suggested that the Serpent Demon send the rug to Queen Anait, for she would pay five hundred pieces of gold for such a weaving.

Several days later, a merchant appeared at the palace gates, insisting that he had a very special carpet to show the queen. When Anait heard of this strange merchant's unusual rug, she frowned. She went out onto her balcony and saw the river roiling and frothing over its banks, dark and dull as iron. The queen strode swiftly from her chambers, her grey eyes glinting. In the great hall she carefully examined the merchant's rug, tracing the pattern of odd markings with her finger. Anait read the words that told of Vatchagan's plight and where he was held captive. Though her heart beat fast, her voice remained calm as she admired the lovely handiwork. When the young queen asked the man where he had found such a fine piece and he gave her no answer, she smiled still.

"You shall be properly rewarded for this rare find. It has cheered me more than you could ever know."

Queen Anait left the great hall and ran to the armory, where she buckled on her sword. She mounted her white stallion and rallied the palace guard with a great cry, and they set off.

Storm clouds raced beside the band of warriors as they galloped across the high plains. They crested the mountain pass as thunder rumbled and lightning cracked the sky. The guards heaved at the boulder blocking the mouth of the cavern. As it rolled away, Queen Anait loosed her sword and rode into the serpent's lair.

The stallion's piercing cries echoed in the cavern as he whirled and reared. Then, from the blackest depths of the mountain, the Serpent Demon came gliding forth. Slowly the huge creature rose up onto his coils, swaying his head to and fro, then drew back to strike. As the serpent lunged at Anait, she plunged her blade into its throat with all of her strength. A single blow was enough. He writhed and lashed his tail till at last he toppled over and lay still.

Anait ran to Vatchagan and released him. The king embraced his queen. "Blessed are you, beloved star of my heart! I knew you would come!"

Anait murmured, "Blessed is the loom that saved your life, dear husband, and blessed are the words I learned to read at your side."

The two lovers returned to their thrones. Once again the vines bore fruit, the ewes suckled their lambs, and the river whispered to itself as it flowed by the palace. To this day, the *ashugs* still sing of their glorious king and queen. And the people of that land still weave the most beautiful rugs in the world.

Three apples fell from heaven—one for you, one for me, and one for all who read this tale.

The first time I read this story I was struck by the maturity of the lovers and their relationship. It's quite unusual for a folktale. Anait's common sense in withholding icy water from her visitor is matched by Vatchagan's humility in accepting Aran's request to learn a trade. His determination to learn to weave is matched by her eagerness to learn to read. He does not hesitate to solicit her advice in ruling the country and she does not hesitate to rescue him by force from the demon. I admire their self-assurance, generosity and healthy devotion to one another.

It's thrilling how deeply Vatchagan trusts Anait—with his very life. Isn't it wonderful how the very thing he taught her is what later saves him? And the craft he learned to win her hand saved his life as well. Although we may never have to depend on our partners to literally save our lives, a successful relationship requires that same depth of trust in one another.

In real life, trust does not always come so easily. At first I was very nervous about accepting help from Tom. I didn't want to risk seeming unknowledgeable or dependent. You can be sure that Tom wasn't too eager to take much advice or assistance from me, either. It took a while for trust to grow, for both of us to feel comfortable receiving aid from the other. Eventually, we discovered that the balance point between independent aloofness and clingy dependence is interdependence. We are stronger when we trust one another's wisdom and accept each other's support.

Wealth, Wisdom, Women

EASTERN EUROPE

Every day Benjamin, Nathan, and Samuel met in the tea shop after work to talk and drink and dream. And every day the young men fell to arguing about what was most necessary to succeed in life.

"You've got to have money, my friends," Benjamin would say firmly. "Money makes the world go round." He'd lean back in his chair and look around at the small, shabby shop. Then Benjamin would declare that if he were a rich man, he'd open an inn and feed everyone, even the poor. Anyone who needed a meal could get one, anytime.

But the second young man always disagreed. Nathan would tap the side of his head and lean forward. "It's wisdom, I tell you. You can't do a thing without learning. You've got to be educated to succeed in this world." Then he'd gaze off with a wistful look in his eyes and say that he'd always wanted to be a scholar. He would open a school and teach children, even poor ones. Yes, he'd let anyone come to his school and share his wisdom with them.

Samuel would nod his head as his friends spoke. "Those are important things, friends, no doubt about it . . . but they're not for me. No. My father, God rest his soul, always told me to marry a good woman. He said that was the best guarantee of happiness *and* success. He said that with a kind, loving wife, a man can do anything in the world." And he'd sit there, lost in his own thoughts.

Whenever Samuel said this, the other two men would look at their companion as if he was crazy, then they'd all laugh at their wishful thinking. They never tired of trying to convince one another of the correctness of their beliefs, and they never changed each other's minds, not even a little.

One day while they sat wrangling and teasing one another, Elijah the prophet came by, disguised as a grey-haired merchant. He asked the young workmen if he might join them and they offered him a chair, for they were brought up to respect their elders. The old fellow asked what they were discussing, and when they told him their dreams, he threw back his head and laughed heartily. Then he looked at them soberly. "But tell me, my young friends," he said, "if you could truly have just one thing in this world, what *would* you wish for?"

Benjamin immediately said, "I'd want money, sir."

Elijah took a small coin out of his pocket and handed it to Benjamin. "Here you are, my son. May you do much good in the world with your fortune."

Nathan said emphatically, "I'd want knowledge, sir."

Elijah reached into his coat and pulled out a small book. "Here you are, my son. May you do much good in the world with your wisdom."

Then Samuel looked into the old merchant's eyes and said simply, "I'd wish for a kind and loving wife, sir."

And Elijah said, "Go home and ask the young woman who lives next door if she will marry you. And may you do much good in the world with your wife."

The grey-haired gentleman excused himself and walked off into the crowded street. In a moment he was lost to sight. The three young fellows stared at each another in wonder for a long moment. Then they fell to arguing about who the stranger might have been and whether he could really grant them their wishes.

Soon enough they found out. Benjamin became a wealthy man and opened an inn known for its delicious food and wine. Coins poured into his moneyboxes and he served everyone a meal, rich and poor alike. Nathan became a scholar of great renown. He opened a school that drew children from the best families, and he offered free teaching to the poor as well. As for Samuel, he married Leah and they set up house together with little more than the clothes on their backs, an old spotted cow, and two happy hearts.

Seven years went by. The three friends no longer gathered at the little shop to talk and drink and dream. But one day a very old, white-bearded man came walking through town and stopped at the elegant inn owned by Benjamin, asking for a hot meal. The innkeeper's servant took one look at the man's patched cloak and scuffed boots and shook his head. "We don't serve beggars anymore. My master says that if you cannot pay, you cannot come in."

Elijah nodded slowly and then asked in a loud voice to see the innkeeper. When Benjamin came to the door and saw the stooped old man, he did not recognize him.

Then the strange fellow accused Benjamin of wasting his wish and demanded his coin back. The wealthy innkeeper was bewildered, but the old man was insistent, so at last Benjamin fished a groshen out of his pocket and tossed it to him with a shrug. "There you are. A coin's a coin in my world, old father. I hope you're satisfied. Now, I have business to attend to." And Benjamin turned away.

From that moment on, his inn fell into decline, and soon Benjamin was a poor and bitter man.

Elijah had a small, ragged child with him when he walked down a broad avenue to an imposing building with a gate around the grounds. He asked the gatekeeper for admission for his grandson into the school. The man sniffed. "My master is a famous scholar. He doesn't waste his time with poor children anymore."

Elijah nodded slowly and then asked in a loud voice to see the great scholar. When Nathan heard the commotion and came to the gate, he did not recognize the bearded old man.

Then the strange fellow accused Nathan of wasting his wish and demanded his book back. The learned teacher was bewildered, but the elderly man was insistent, so at last Nathan pulled a small textbook out of his coat pocket and handed it to him with a shrug. "There you are. A book's a book in my world, old father. I hope you're satisfied. Now, I have students to attend to." And Nathan turned away.

From that moment on, his academy fell into disrepute, and soon Nathan was an idle and bitter man.

At the outskirts of town, a dusty traveler paused beside a field of barley, where two young men were reaping. The white-bearded fellow called to ask if they had any water to share.

"There is plenty of water, old father, at the home of our mistress. If you'll go round the bend to her house, Mistress Leah will give you a cup of water—and anything else besides if you ask for it."

"And does your Mistress Leah have a husband?"

"Oh, to be sure, old father, that is our master, Samuel. You will find him in the barn."

"And does he pay you well, my sons?"

The reapers smiled and shook their heads. "We could make more money at another farm, old sir, but we like it here. Mistress Leah is kind to us, and Master Samuel is fair. We will always be well cared for as long as we work for them."

The young men lifted their scythes and fell to work again. The old man watched them for awhile and then walked on. He saw two young women picking apples from old trees heavy with fruit and asked them if they had a crust of bread to spare. One of the girls curtsied and spoke. "We've nothing but apples here, old father, but our mistress feeds us dinner soon and I'm sure she would feed you as well. There is a saying in Mistress Leah's house, 'There's always enough to feed one more.'"

The other girl handed him a plump, rosy apple and the stranger smiled when he tasted it.

"Mistress Leah cares for these trees, old father. The fruit was pocked and sour when she came to this farm. See how she has given them new life."

The white-haired traveler nodded and then walked on, stopping before a small house. Flowers bloomed along the path to the door and two children romped with a dog in the yard. Behind the house there was a weathered shed, a vegetable patch, and a pasture with three goats and a spotted cow. A woman came to the door and greeted him cheerfully. She offered him a chair before the fire to rest and warm himself. As the old man drank a mug of water, he peered around the tiny, crowded room.

Loaves of freshly baked bread cooled on a bare wooden table, and bunches of herbs and garlic and onions hung overhead. Leah gently corrected a young boy scrawling in an exercise book with his pen, while her fingers flew over a half-knitted cap.

Soon Samuel came in from the barn, the workers came in from the fields and orchard, and they all squeezed around the table. The master gave thanks for their food, for their health, for the good weather, for their visitor. And last of all, he thanked God for his greatest blessing, his wife Leah. Then they ate a whole pot of chicken stew, to the last bite.

After the meal, Samuel tarried with his guest. Their talk turned to a man's dreams and what a man must do to make those dreams come true.

"And have your dreams come true, my son?"

Samuel laughed. "More sweetly than I could have ever imagined. You know, when I was a young man full of wild hopes, a stranger appeared to me and my friends. He gave Benjamin a coin, and he became a wealthy innkeeper; he gave Nathan a book, and he became a scholar. To me, he gave only a piece of advice. He said I should marry the woman who lived next door. That was Leah. She has been the joy of my life, old father. I have often wished that I might meet that gentleman again, to thank him for my good fortune . . . But what of your dreams, sir? Surely you have had many dreams in your life."

The white-bearded guest smiled at Samuel and called Leah to his side. Holding their hands, he spoke quietly.

"Seeing you two and the lives you lead, this is my dream come true, for I am that stranger you heeded so many years ago."

Then Elijah drew from his coat pocket a groshen and a small book and handed them to Samuel and Leah. "My children, may you be blessed with wealth and wisdom for the rest of your days."

From that moment on, the couple prospered and grew rich, their children never knew sorrow or hunger, and they were praised throughout the land for their generous hearts. To the end of his days Samuel was a happy and grateful man.

The Jewish culture has always fostered a strong sense of responsibility among couples to perform acts of kindness and charity. Many of their folktales reflect this belief in mitzvot. *In this story we see the beauty of a couple who are devoted to one another and to the greater good.*

Samuel's recognition that loving partnership—instead of material gain or personal achievement—is the foundation of happiness and success can be a reminder to us all that our relationships can truly be our life work. Imagine approaching commitment from this perspective! In the face of rampant self-centeredness and the dismal divorce rate, you could strengthen your community by the simple act of nurturing and maintaining your relationship, acting as a model of partnership. Please believe me, other couples will notice your commitment and take heart from it.

One Hundred Coins

FUJIAN, CHINA

They were like the wild geese, those birds that mate for life, Aming and his wife Axiu. Never was there a couple more constant and true. Together they tilled and planted their mountainside fields and sweated beneath the merciless sun; together they rose before dawn to toss out their fishnets and later pull their catch on board. Like a team of oxen, harnessed to the same plow, their neighbors said. Like a pair of dolphins that rise from the waves as one.

But misfortune befalls even the most devoted of couples. One day in the season of monsoons, Axiu was out cutting firewood when she was caught in a drenching downpour. By the time she found her way home, Axiu was blue-lipped and trembling. And though Aming nursed her with steaming licorice root tea, she was soon delirious. She lay feverish at night and shivering beneath her quilt by day, feebly shaking her head even at bowls of rice gruel.

Aming hovered over his wife, feeding her broth and tea, placing poultices on her chest, wiping her burning cheeks with cool cloths. As the weeks stretched on, Aming grew weary, but he remained faithfully at her side until once more Axiu returned his smiles.

As autumn approached, the couple found themselves deeply in debt, with little hope of paying the herb doctor, the village grocer, or the man who had cut firewood for them.

Aming was an honorable man. He swore stoutly that he'd repay the debts, no matter how large. But their fields had flooded, and there was little enough rice for themselves; there was none to sell. As time passed, many young men in Tangshan village left the country to seek work elsewhere. When one of them mentioned jobs to be had in Singapore, Aming considered this.

Now Aming and Axiu always put their heads together on such matters, so the young husband took his thoughts to his beloved wife. Her eyes grew wide and filled with tears.

"No, my dearest. Singapore is so far away. What if something happened to you?"

A day passed, and the herb doctor pressed Aming for payment. Again he broached the subject, but Axiu frowned and shook her head. "No, I have heard from other women that their husbands are treated badly there. I couldn't bear to think of you being beaten or robbed—or worse."

But when a week passed and their rice sacks were almost empty, Aming mentioned Singapore a third time. Axiu sighed and bowed her head. "Very well, my love, but your going will break my heart."

On the morning that he set off for the harbor, Axiu wept and hugged him tightly. "I will pray every day for your safe passage over the sea, Aming, but how will I know when you arrive? Please send a message."

"You know I cannot write, Axiu. But I'll find a way."

Both of them sent forth many prayers to the sea goddess Mazu while Aming sailed south across the vast ocean, and Axiu made offerings at her temple. In Singapore, Aming toiled in the steaming rice fields, pulled carts laden with fruit, and hauled bulging nets from the sea. Night after night he fell asleep exhausted, only to rise at first light, gulp a bowl of rice, and go back down to the port to hire himself out again. Always he thought of his wife and pined for her, but he had no time for letters.

Finally Aming bought writing supplies and painted one figure on a sheet of paper. He carefully folded the letter and sent it home with a villager returning to Tangshan. Axiu opened the letter with shaking hands and saw a picture of one wild goose. Her heart ached with love as she sent back a drawing of one lone tree.

Winter passed. Aming wanted to settle his accounts before the Spring Festival. He had saved one hundred silver coins to send to Axiu, but he hesitated to send them so far away. He wondered who he could trust to safely transport such a great sum. And how could he let his wife know how much money to expect?

Now, Chen San had sailed from Tangshan with the other young men, but he soon found the hard labor distasteful. Instead he made his money travelling back and forth from the village to Singapore entrusted with letters, money, and other valuables that were exchanged between the villagers and their missing loved ones. Whenever he could, he pinched a few coins from the unsuspecting poor folk, and in this way he was satisfied with his lot.

Just before the festival, Chen San arrived at Axiu's home with a heavy sack of coins and a letter for her. The scoundrel had opened the letter and had been amused to find that it was nothing more than paintings of animals, no words at all. He chuckled at the foolish peasants he tricked so easily.

Axiu welcomed Chen San into her home and peppered him with questions. Was Aming well, was he happy, what did he say, what was it like living in Singapore? Chen San replied vaguely with answers that he thought she might like to hear, then handed over the sack with a flourish. Axiu flushed at the sight of so much money; it was more than she had ever seen before. Then she read Aming's letter and her heart sank with misgiving.

Carefully she counted out the coins and stacked them in piles before she spoke to her fellow villager. "Elder Brother, I am indeed grateful for your news and for bringing this money to me, but I think there has been a mistake. Shouldn't there be one hundred silver coins in this pouch? I count only fifty."

The rogue wondered how this simple-minded woman could have guessed the truth. He insisted that he had been given only fifty coins and that he had delivered them all to her as agreed.

Axiu looked at the letter again and was certain that she was being cheated. Though he blustered and threatened and denied her accusations, the young woman kept pressing him till finally Chen San suggested that they let the village elder settle their dispute. Axiu told her story; Chen San told his. Many of the villagers gathered round and agreed that Chen San was reliable in bringing money from their husbands and brothers across the sea. The village elder scratched his head and frowned at Axiu.

He asked for proof that Aming had sent her one hundred coins, since even the strongest men had never sent their families more than fifty.

The young wife trembled as she pulled the letter from her tunic and unfolded it on the table before the elder. As her neighbors whispered and chuckled among themselves, Axiu prayed that he saw the same message she did.

"My Uncle, Aming has drawn me four dogs. Now, 'dog' sounds like 'nine,' yes? So nine fours make thirty-six. And then he's drawn eight turtles. We know that 'turtle' sounds like 'eight,' correct? There are eight of them, so I make that out to be sixty-four. And when I add thirty-six and sixty-four, Honored Uncle, it is one hundred. My husband cannot write, but he is telling me plainly that he has sent one hundred silver coins, no more, no less. This man has stolen half of the money my husband worked so hard to earn!"

The elder turned to Chen San and looked him in the eye. "If you cannot swear before Mazu that you are innocent, you had better deliver those coins now."

Chen San turned pale. When a man makes his living sailing back and forth across the seas he does not dare to risk his life by lying to the sea goddess. He stood speechless, gaping first at Axiu and then the village elder. At last Chen San shook himself and spoke.

"Little Sister, forgive me for my error. So many depend upon me to carry their valuables that I must have become confused. You are right, I have made a mistake. I will bring you the rest of your money now."

And so, when Chen San journeyed again to Singapore, he sought out Aming first of all and told him that his debts had been paid in full. Aming marveled at this news, for he did not think that he had sent enough money. But Chen San only replied dryly, "Sometimes the great Mazu comes to our aid, Brother, when we least expect it." Then he handed the young husband a letter from Axiu. Aming cried with joy as he looked at the brush strokes on the paper. Curious in spite of himself, Chen San glanced down at the letter. There he saw two wild geese, touching wing to wing, flying toward their mountain home.

The simple courage and perseverance that Aming and Axiu demonstrate in this story isn't the stuff of breathless romance novels or lighthearted comedy films. It is the truth of couplehood, though. Day-to-day support and unwavering love is what makes relationships taste sweeter than the rarest vintage wine.

In this portrait of a companionate marriage, Aming and Axiu stand side by side, united by mutual respect, faith, and common goals. They have learned the necessity of sacrifice and compromise in the face of difficulties. I have the sense that they will never be materially wealthy, but the richness of their partnership is a treasure beyond compare.

The Linden and the Oak

GREECE

Long ago, in the rocky hill country of Phrygia, far from towns and temples and people, two trees grew from a single trunk. It is not unusual for a pair of sycamores or pines to grow together thus, but these two were an oak and a linden. And some of the old hillfolk in that wild and solitary land could tell you a tale of how those two trees came to be.

⌐⋎⌐

Baucis and Philemon had been together for so long, they had lost count of the years. It seemed that they had always lived in a little hut among the hills, tending their gardens, pressing olives, milking goats, and herding geese.

They were poor, very poor. When they were younger and stronger, Philemon had planted large fields and Baucis had kept a herd of goats. But as they grew old, the couple could not do the work themselves and in all the country round them, no one offered to help, so they learned to do without. Still, Baucis and Philemon were content.

Though the land of Phrygia boasted thriving towns and wealthy farmers, there were few that went to bed each night with greater peace of mind. The old couple was happy because they had each other. Philemon was ever mindful to thank Zeus for their health and good fortune, while Baucis did not forget to thank Hera for the blessing of their marriage.

One afternoon in late spring when the sun warmed their old bones, Baucis cut stalks of lavender from her herb beds and Philemon rubbed leaves of lemon balm inside a new beehive. Baucis chuckled. "Listen to us, husband, we are both humming, like a couple of your old bees."

Philemon looked at her and smiled. In his eyes, Baucis would always be beautiful. She would always be his dark-eyed, laughing lover with soft curves and full lips. "I am humming because I am coming to taste your nectar, wife!"

They embraced beneath the cloudless sky and Baucis ran her hands through his tangled grey curls as they kissed.

The couple spent the day working in their garden. As the sun chariot headed for the far western hills, they rested for a moment, breathing in the scent of wild roses, listening to the doves murmuring to one another. Then Baucis went inside to prepare their evening meal while Philemon saw to the goat.

There was little enough to eat, for their store of winter provisions was nearly gone and the new garden was still young. As Baucis measured out a tiny portion of ground meal, Philemon brought in a scanty bucket of milk. He was just blowing up the coals of the fire when he heard a knock on the door. The two old people turned and looked at one another in surprise. No one had been to their hut since an old neighbor had come to ask Philemon's advice about bees, and that man had been dead ten winters or more.

At the second knock, Baucis opened the door and saw two strangers in stained, faded cloaks and worn leather sandals. She peered up at the two men and smiled warmly, opening the weather-beaten door wide. Philemon stepped to her side, smiling as well.

"Welcome to our home, brothers. We are honored to have you as our guests."

It had been many years since the couple had entertained anyone, but they had not forgotten the sacred rules of courtesy to a guest. They set about making their visitors comfortable and then scoured that little hut for the makings of a meal. In the dim firelight, they moved rickety benches close to the table, covered the worn wood with goatskins, and offered a bowl of warm water for their guests to wash off the dust of the road. Baucis rubbed fresh mint leaves on the rough, plank table, then she put their last olives into a bowl for the men. Philemon slipped outside and plucked the very first radishes for them.

As they bustled about, Baucis and Philemon paused to exchange pleased glances. They laughed together as they struggled to retrieve a hunk of bacon from their only ham hanging in the rafters. Baucis's kind old heart beat faster as their guests praised the pungency of the radishes from her husband's garden, the plumpness of the olives from his grove. When the men commented on the aroma coming from the pot hung over the fire, Philemon gave a nod, and Baucis added the last of their onions and cabbage and the rest of the grain. He whispered that all would be well; the gods would take care of them.

After asking for Father Zeus's blessing on the meal, Philemon served his guests and then confided that he was certain the gods on high did not enjoy as tasty a stew as his dear Baucis had made. The two strangers laughingly concurred.

Those travelers must have been very hungry for they did not refuse second helpings. When the pot was empty, Baucis set out a wooden dish of fresh honeycomb. She watched their faces as they tasted the honey and proudly told them of Philemon's skill with bees. They marveled at its delicate sweetness and asked his secret.

"Why, it's the lemon balm my Baucis grows outside our door. The bees love it best of all." Philemon winked at his wife. The guests looked at one another, then glanced around the room. It would not have surprised them to see Aphrodite lurking in one of the darkened corners.

But Baucis disagreed. "Nonsense, my dear. It's you they love best of all. You dote on them so. There is a grove of linden trees not far from here and every spring Philemon moves the hives over to those trees when the linden blossoms are in flower. That's what makes our honey so sweet." Then she leaned forward, eager to ask her guests for news of the great world she no longer visited.

The food disappeared in due course, but the wine bowl continued to brim full. And the wine itself, watery and a bit sour at first, became richer and mellower each time Philemon refilled their beechwood cups. When Baucis noticed this, she opened her mouth to tease Philemon for hoarding the best wine. Then it dawned on her that the true cause of this transformation had nothing to do with Philemon or their grapes.

Slowly she turned to look more closely at the two strangers sharing her table. As the older, taller one met her gaze, she realized who he was. He smiled at her tenderly and nodded, as if to assure her that all was well. Baucis grabbed Philemon's arm and shook it, pointing wordlessly to the wine and then to their guests. His jaw sagged and his cup clattered onto the table when he understood her meaning. The old couple begged pardon, bowing and apologizing for offering such a paltry meal to their immortal guests.

Zeus spoke kindly. "Faithful friends, I have never had such a delightful meal, not even on Olympus's heights. Your hospitality has been impeccable, and your reverence is refreshing."

Then he beckoned for them to follow him outside. Baucis and Philemon cried out in astonishment. In the fading light, they saw that all of the countryside around them had been swallowed up by water. Their neighbors' huts, the villages in the valley below, the distant town—nothing remained. In a somber voice, Zeus told them that he and Hermes had been treated rudely by those who had forgotten the laws of hospitality. The couple murmured in sorrow as they gazed over the flooded land. Then they turned and looked back at their own tiny hut. It too had disappeared, but in its place stood a majestic temple of polished white marble with a roof of burnished gold.

"Baucis, Philemon, I will grant any request that you ask of me as reward for your piety and faithfulness."

The old husband and wife whispered together for a few moments. Then Philemon said, "Great Zeus, we ask only two things. May we spend the rest of our lives as stewards of your temple here. And since we have lived together so long, we ask that we never be parted. May we both die at the same time."

Their wishes were fulfilled. The two old people lived in comfort and splendor, tending the temple fires, offering sacrifices and worshipping Father Zeus. Then one day, when they had forgotten how many years they had cared for the temple, they walked out onto the hillside.

Baucis and Philemon stood in the bright sunshine of late spring, holding hands, looking out over the country below. They talked of many things, remembering their long and happy life together. Baucis felt her feet on the warm, firm earth. Philemon felt the breeze brushing against his arms, through his hair. They both breathed in the scent of wild roses and sighed in deep contentment.

The lovers fell silent and then slowly their feet took root, holding them in place. Their bodies thickened, covered with grey and brown bark. Their arms and heads were crowned with branches full of leaves that rustled in the breeze. They had only time to say farewell before they were transformed. Growing from the same trunk, they became a towering oak and a flowering linden. That day, Philemon's bees found a new linden tree where none had been before. They swarmed over its cream-colored blossoms and covered themselves with pollen, then returned to their hives.

And that is the story of Baucis and Philemon, the linden and the oak. From that time on, in the hill country of Phrygia, it is said that the bees made the sweetest honey from the linden trees that grew there, honey so sweet that even the everlasting gods on Mount Olympus loved it best of all.

Baucis and Philemon have attained what every couple longs for in their union. They are fulfilled, living every day in gratitude and appreciation. They would readily agree with the Vietnamese concept of marriage as a "hundred-year friendship."

I believe that their devotion to Spirit is the secret of their satisfaction, for every successful relationship has a third partner, another Presence that suffuses it with grace. It is called by many names—Guiding Spirit, Holy Mother Goddess, Jesus, Guardian Angel. When a couple welcomes and honors that Presence, their life together is transformed. Something greater than their own efforts works to shape, strengthen, and bless the union.

Sometimes you will feel overwhelmed by all the difficulties of life piled on your doorstep like an unwanted clutch of snapping turtles. Sometimes your heart will ache when you realize the dreams you shared will never come true. Sometimes you might even forget why you ever loved your partner. In those moments, trusting that you will be cared for by the third Presence in your relationship may help more than anything you can do yourselves. Have faith.

When Peter Churned the Butter

NORWAY

Elsa and Peter had a snug little farm with a cow in the barn, hay in the loft, and a babe on the floor just learning how to crawl. Elsa did the cooking and baking, the washing and tidying up. Peter worked all day in the fields, plowing and planting, hoeing and harvesting.

Every evening when Peter returned from his work, the house was clean, Sophie was asleep in her cradle, and supper was hot on the table. Peter began to wonder what it was that Elsa did to keep herself busy all day. It didn't seem fair that she never had to swing a scythe, never got her nose choked with dust or her neck scratched with chaff, and had the animals and baby for company the whole day through. He began to grumble about things.

One night, he made up his mind to do something. He cleared his throat, banged his ale mug on the table—and woke up the baby.

"Elsa, it seems to me that something's not right here. I spend the livelong day out in the blistering sun, raising calluses on my hands and grubbing in the weeds till my back is half broken. But every night when I come home, you're singing and smiling and putting a jug of flowers on the table. Seems to me you're not working half as hard as I am, wife, and I don't like it!"

Elsa shushed their wailing daughter and stared at her husband. She opened her mouth two or three times to say something, but thought better of it. At last she smiled sweetly and put her hand on her husband's arm.

"Well, now, my dear, is that how things seem to you? No wonder you're so grumpy these days. Whatever shall we do?"

Peter frowned and blinked for a moment. Then he blustered, "Let *me* stay home for a change and tend the house. I dare say I can do all the chores you do and then some. You try your hand at the mowing for awhile. What do you say?"

Elsa agreed, and the next morning she kissed little Sophie, shouldered the scythe, and waved to Peter. "Now, all you need do is churn some butter, tether the cow in her pasture, and grind some grain for our noonday porridge. Oh, and mind the baby, dear, she's partial to the pig. I'll be back when the sun is overhead."

Peter chuckled to himself. "Just as I thought—a dab of churning, a spot of grinding, and a stroll to the pasture. Why, I'll be done in no time. Perhaps I'll sit here in the sun and smoke a pipe before I get to work."

He filled his pipe and settled down for a leisurely smoke. Then he spied Sophie crawling into the pigpen. By the time Peter scooped her out of the muck, she was brown and smelly from head to toe.

Peter tucked Sophie under his arm and hauled a bucket of water from the well. He filled the kettle and blew up the fire in the hearth. Sophie's shift and booties and Peter's shirt were so filthy he decided to wash them, and then he decided he'd do all of the other washing as well.

Sophie wiggled as he tried to undress her. She squirmed as he filled a basin with steamy water and dipped her in it. She shrieked at the scalding hot water and her father hopped around the room, blowing on her red bottom and trying to quiet her squalls.

Peter had seen Elsa rub butter on her fingers when she burned them so he looked around for the butter dish and that reminded him of the churning yet to be done. He tossed the pan of hot water out the door and rinsed the baby off with a stream of cold water out of the bucket. Sophie howled. Her father put a clean shift on her and set her on the floor. "Now mind you don't go far," he warned her as he plopped all of the dirty clothes into the big kettle of water over the fire.

Certain that he had everything well in hand, Peter settled down to the churning with a will. Before too long he fancied that he'd worked up a thirst and thought he'd get himself a stout mug of ale from the barrel in the cellar. But as he crossed the room and looked out the door, he spied his daughter. She had crawled back to the pigpen and pulled herself up on the wooden gate so she could give the pig a kiss.

Peter grabbed the child and wiped her face clean. He stuck Sophie in her cradle and wrapped the blankets around her tightly. Then he went through the trapdoor and down into the cellar, unplugged the bunghole, and listened to the satisfying gluggle of the ale as it poured into his mug. He was smacking his lips, already enjoying his drink, when he heard a thump and a wail up above him.

Peter took the steps three at a time, certain something terrible had happened to Sophie. He left the mug under the spout and the bung in his hand. The baby had fallen out of the cradle, still wrapped in her thick woolen blankets, so she was unharmed, but the thump had come when the pig had knocked over the churn.

The pig was happily lapping up cream when Peter rushed at him—and slipped on the thick layer of liquid that covered the floor. Peter's legs flew up into the air and he landed right on top of the pig. The animal had the wind knocked clean out of him.

After Peter picked up the babe and changed his shirt, he went to the barn and got more cream. He hoisted the full churn onto his back and then he saw the cow, still standing in her stall. "I'll just water the cow while I'm out here," he thought. He went to the well, lowered the bucket and filled it, then leaned over to haul the bucket out. Cream spilled out of the top of the churn and into the well water, running all over his hair and into his eyes and ears. As he sputtered and licked his lips, he realized that he was still thirsty.

Then he remembered the ale barrel. The *open* ale barrel. Peter sprinted to the house but skidded to a stop in the doorway. The pig had recovered; he and Sophie were now rolling in the cream. With a groan, he grabbed his slippery child, poured cold water over her again, and put on the first shift he could lay hands on. He let the pig lick the floor clean while he set Sophie under the table to play with some wooden spoons.

The spoons reminded him of eating, eating soup . . . stew . . . porridge . . . Porridge! He still had to grind the grain for the noonday meal! The oats were soft, easily ground, and he soon had a decent bowlful on the table.

He noticed that the fire had died down, so he knelt before it, coaxing the coals back to life with fresh wood. Meanwhile, Sophie crawled out from under the table and pulled herself up on a chair leg. Peter turned around just as she tipped the entire bowl of oatmeal onto her head. The little girl howled indignantly as she was doused with the last of the cold water. Peter put another shift on her and then went outside to fetch another bucketful of water.

Drawing water from the well reminded Peter of the cow. The poor cow! Never fed, never watered, inside her stall the entire morning. It was much too late to think of taking her all the way to the pasture. But Peter had noticed that there was plenty of fresh green grass on the sod-covered roof of their home. He decided he would let the cow graze there.

It was a simple enough decision, but getting the animal onto the roof was a bit of a job. The cow was unreasonably balky, Peter thought. She adamantly refused to get onto the plank he had laid down for her from the steep hillside next to the cottage, across open space and onto the top of the house. Only after he enticed her with his cap full of oats did she clamber across. Peter was a dutiful farmer; he tied a long rope onto the cow's collar, slipped the other end down the chimney, scrambled down from the roof, and tied the rope round his waist. He was certain he would feel her tugging and could come out to assist her if anything should go amiss.

Of course, the oats for the cow reminded him of the porridge for his family. The sun was climbing high in the sky as he ground up more grain, dumped it in the kettle, and then . . . wondered where the baby was. He looked under the table and the bed, in her cradle and the clothes chest, and then he saw the open cellar door in the corner. Sophie had rolled down the steps and landed in a bed of soft mud, the earthen floor of the cellar mixed with a full keg of ale. She was filthy but unhurt. Peter had no more clothes to put on her so he wiped her off as best he could and set her down outside in the sun to dry off. The pig, drunk on cream, waddled over to Sophie's side and collapsed with a grunt.

As Elsa neared home, she heard the cow bawling desperately. She broke into a run when she saw the animal dangling from the roof by a rope tied to her collar. Elsa swung her scythe and sliced the rope so that the cow flopped to the ground, with her eyes rolled back in her head. Sophie sat in front of the house naked, muddy, with her father's pipe stuck in her mouth, smelling like beer. She was snuggled up against the sleeping pig, its jowls greasy and belly swollen from a churnful of cream.

Elsa took a deep breath and looked inside the house. The floor was slick with butterfat, the cellar door gaped open, the whole place reeked of ale—and Peter was wedged in the chimney, where he'd been jerked when the cow fell from the roof. He was hanging head down over the bubbling kettle.

Elsa pushed the kettle out of the way, pulled Peter out of the chimney, and dusted him off with her apron. Then she wiped off Sophie and wrapped her in a blanket. Peter slumped on a chair with the baby in his lap while Elsa set the table.

"Well, at least we have porridge to eat," she said cheerfully.

Elsa stirred up the oatmeal with her big wooden ladle—and fished out a little shirt. Next, she brought up one of Peter's woolen socks, then a diaper, all dripping with clots of oatmeal.

Elsa glanced over at her husband. "Shall I go back to the fields after lunch, dear, and finish up the cutting?"

Peter lurched out of his chair, and the baby wailed as she hit the floor. "No, no! I'll go!"

That evening, when Peter returned from his work, the house was clean, the baby was fast asleep in her cradle (entirely worn out from her day's adventures) and supper was already served up, hot on the table. Peter dug into a steaming bowl of vegetable soup. He gulped it down without a pause, till at the bottom of the bowl he scraped up a sodden woolen bootie.

He looked up at Elsa. She smiled. Not a word was ever said about that morning, but Peter never complained about his share of the work again.

Is there a single one of us who hasn't fantasized about trading places with someone else for a day? Someone whose life seems to be more romantic, more relaxed, more glamourous, more fulfilling than our own? Over the years, I find myself increasingly grateful for my own lot in life, even though I'd still like to trade places with someone who is more organized than I am.

Several years ago, Tom and I decided that our shared life needed more organization. Too many dates and duties and opportunities were slipping by, undone or unnoticed. How did we respond to this dilemma? We made lists! Comprehensive lists. Not of the acute, do-it-this-week variety; no, we were trying to get an overview on how to maintain a household, our child, and our relationship, all in one document.

It took a while, but we itemized every area of our life and discussed how to divide up the responsibilities. That was a fine moment for us. We created this master plan together and were duly impressed with our own individual contributions. We were also grateful for the sizable commitments our partner had made.

But when we finished, we knew that we had gained something much more significant than an itemization of who would pay the bills or schedule our dental appointments. As we worked on our master plan, we began to recognize all of the essential but intangible contributions we make to our life together. That realization was humbling, heartening, and inspiring. To this day, we regularly acknowledge how much we each bring to this relationship, how well we complement each other. There is no question in our minds; we're a good pair. Now, if we could just find those lists . . .

Reflections on a Marriage

JAPAN

Kizen and Sachido married in the spring, and they had eyes for nothing but each other. When Kizen left in the mornings to cut bamboo, there were so many sighs and kisses and assurances of love that sometimes the sun cleared the mountainside and shone into their little valley before they finished their good-byes. When Kizen returned in the evenings, the kissing and embracing and whispering went on till the owls hooted in the forest nearby. This is to be expected when you are young, when your love is new.

One day Kizen learned that he must make a trip into the capital to settle some business. He had walked many times to the village on the far side of the mountain where he sold his bamboo, but no further. Traveling down into the capital city of their province, now that was an adventure he had never had before! It would be a day's journey to the city, a day to conduct his business, then a day returning home. Sachido warned him to watch for pickpockets, while his friends urged him to try some of the wines in the marketplace. Kizen didn't know if he should be excited or frightened. All he was certain of was that he would miss his wife terribly.

At last a day dawned that was favorable for undertaking such a journey. The young couple wept and sighed and clung to one another till the sun burned high in the sky. Finally he set off down the trail, and she stood waving a scarf till he was out of sight.

Sachido had packed enough food for her husband to walk to Mount Fuji and back. Kizen trudged along for hours, sweating under the burden of the sack slung over his shoulder. It never occurred to him to discard even a morsel, for his devoted wife had prepared it for him. Toward nightfall he reached the great city and made his way to the inn his friends had recommended.

In the morning Kizen appeared, trembling, before a magistrate, but the matter was eventually settled to his advantage and the young bamboo cutter left the official's chambers surprised and pleased. Blinking in the bright noonday sun, Kizen wondered what he should do. He thought of setting off for home immediately, arriving unexpectedly. The young man grinned as he imagined how his wife would squeal in delight and throw her arms around him.

Then he remembered what his friends had told him, of the astonishing sights and delectable treats of the marketplace. Kizen felt the small pouch of coins tucked inside his kimono. He had enough money to buy a cup of *sake* for himself and a gift to surprise Sachido. So he wandered off, following his nose, until he found the great marketplace at the center of the city.

Never had Kizen seen such wonders! Bolts of silk the color of the sunset, chopsticks carved with dragons, buckets of fish that gleamed golden even in the shade. He wandered from one end of the market to the other. After hours of gawking, his heart jumped. As people bustled by all around him the young peasant stood dumbstruck, for there, propped up on a table in a stall, was a painting nestled in a small round frame—and it was a portrait of his revered, dead father!

Incredible as it seemed, there was no doubt in Kizen's mind; it *was* his father. The painting depicted him as a young man, as Kizen recalled him from his childhood. He could not remember when his father had ever left their home in the mountains and traveled to the city, but here was certain proof that he had come to the great capital where someone had painted his likeness. Eagerly he paid for the small, silvered disk and selected a gaily lacquered comb for his wife as well.

Kizen set off at daybreak, stopping only once beside a stream to drink and eat some of his dear wife's provisions. Then he continued on, puffing and sweating, anxious to see the look on Sachido's face when he presented her with his gift. The sun was still glowing on the distant peaks behind him when Kizen walked through his village toward his hut.

Sachido ran to greet him and they held one another till the moon rose. At last they stumbled up the path to their house and then, seated before their hearth, Kizen gave his wife the comb. The riches of an emperor's treasure room could not have pleased her more, and Kizen fell asleep that night with a well-contented smile on his lips.

The next morning, Kizen carefully unwrapped his father's portrait and placed it on the altar in the family shrine. He was so pleased to be gazing upon his father's face again that he lingered long over his morning devotions. After bidding Sachido a tender farewell, he hiked up the mountain to cut bamboo.

Every day Kizen communed happily with his father's spirit, peering raptly at the portrait of the dead man. Sometimes, with his head bowed in reverence, he would speak to his honorable father, telling him his hopes and troubles. Though he did not realize it, Kizen's visits with the ancestors grew longer and longer while his affectionate farewells to his wife became shorter and shorter.

Sachido began to wonder why her husband was spending so much time in the family shrine. She wanted to know who he was speaking to for such long periods of time. She missed his ardent embraces and fevered kisses. One day, after Kizen had set off for the bamboo groves, Sachido opened the shrine and peeked in. There in the center of the altar she saw a gleaming silver disk. Charmed by its beauty, she picked up the lovely frame to admire the carving around its edge. Imagine her shock and dismay when she found herself looking at the face of a very pretty, smiling young woman!

The love in a new bride's heart is a fragile thing, easily crushed. And the same flame that feeds her devotion can turn to a raging fire of jealousy in a heartbeat. No sooner did Sachido see this other woman's face than she hated her. No sooner did she discover this other woman hidden in her husband's shrine than she despised him.

Shrieking and wailing, she ran down the path to her parents' home. Sachido flung herself into her mother's arms, blurting out the discovery of her husband's infidelity. This was quite bewildering to the young woman's mother, who had overheard the two lovers swearing their undying devotion to each other just that morning.

"What causes you to think Kizen is unfaithful to you, my dear?"

"I have found his lover! He keeps a portrait of her hidden in our shrine. See, here she is!" The young wife shoved the silver frame into her mother's hands. Looking where her daughter pointed, Sachido's mother saw a wrinkled, grey-haired old woman.

"Well! What a fool your husband is, to leave you, fresh and fair as a peach blossom, for a withered old hag. Why, she's lost half her teeth too! Whatever could he be thinking? I tell you, my dear, you're better off without the likes of *him!*"

It didn't take more to convince Sachido; she was ready to leave the lout then and there. Shouting indignantly, Kizen's wife and her mother marched off to the magistrate where Sachido demanded a divorce from her husband on the grounds of infidelity. When the judge asked for evidence of the charge, Sachido shoved the silver framed disk into his hands.

"There, most venerable sir, see for yourself. I found this hidden in our family shrine this morning. He spends hours in there every day, talking and whispering, yet he barely kisses me goodbye anymore," she sniffed.

The magistrate looked down at the shining surface and saw a plump, jowly fellow with beady black eyes. "Is this your idea of a joke? You two women come here and disrupt my court to mock me with paintings of fat old men? Get out of here before I order both of you flogged!" He shoved the portrait into Sachido's hands, and the mother and daughter ran off down the street, babbling in confusion.

The women and children who heard their clamor clustered round them in curiosity, pelting them with questions and tossing in their opinions on the matter. Hearing the uproar, one of the old men of the village ran off to find Kizen. Soon the young man joined his wife and mother-in-law in front of his hut.

When he asked what the trouble was, Sachido thrust the painting under his nose. "*This* is the matter, you faithless snake. Spending all of your time with *her* instead of me."

Kizen looked down at the portrait of his father, who appeared a bit more surprised than he usually did. The young husband tried his best to convince Sachido that the portrait was a likeness of his dear, dead father, not some strange woman who had stolen his heart. Sachido cried, "What do you think I am—a fool? I know a woman's face when I see one. And she's a beauty. Of *course* you would rather be with her than me." As she began to sob again her mother scolded him for lying to her daughter.

At last, the man who had fetched Kizen from the bamboo forest suggested that they seek advice from the old nun in the convent on the hill. She had once lived for many years in the great capital and was known to be very wise. Everyone in the village followed Kizen and Sachido and her mother as they trotted along, fussing and sniping and sniffling. The elderly nun received them kindly and ushered the three into her private chambers.

Kizen explained how he had found this remarkable painting of his father as a young man in the marketplace of the capital, and then how he had simply placed it in the family shrine out of respect and devotion. But his wife kept interrupting, calling him a liar, insisting that it was a picture of a beautiful young woman whom he had met in the city and who was undoubtedly awaiting the right moment to replace her. Then Sachido's mother piped up and said she really didn't think the woman was such a beauty, and furthermore she was shocked that Kizen would insult his young wife by bringing home another woman so old and homely.

The nun sat quietly, nodding her head to each in turn. When everyone had run out of breath, she asked to see the silver-rimmed portrait and then dismissed them all from her presence for a moment. Standing outside her door, Kizen thought he heard a muffled noise from within, perhaps coughing or chanting, but everything was so confusing that he couldn't be sure.

Soon she summoned them back into her chamber.

"Dear ones, I have meditated on this person who has caused you so much pain and I have decided that it would be best for all concerned if the, *ahem*, portrait stays here and becomes a part of our order. I personally shall see to it that no further distress comes to any of you on its account.

"Remember, dear ones, do not put your faith in illusions, no matter how well they may be crafted. The truth lies in what your own hearts know. Now, please forgive one another and go home in peace."

When the young couple and Sachido's mother had left the cloister, the old woman chuckled and shook her head. She walked over to a large sandalwood chest and lifted out a pile of quilts and robes. Reaching down into its fragrant depths, she gently placed the shining silver disk on top of the last folded garment. And just before she covered it over with the rest of the clothing and blankets, from the bottom of the chest an old nun winked and grinned up at her.

My guess is that anyone who has ever invested his or her heart in a relation-ship has had an unwelcome visit from Jealousy at one time or another. One moment you're purring with pleasure, the next you hear a furtive knock on your door. If you open it, even a crack, Jealousy will slither right in and take aim straight at your innocent, unsuspecting heart. Frequently, Jealousy's boon companion, Rage, shows up on your doorstep, too, and then you're really in trouble.

Jealousy and Rage work fast, too fast. Reason and Trust are trampled outside on the garden path when Jealousy and Rage come stampeding into your home. They are superb illusionists, throwing lifelike shadows into every corner, warping the mir-rors to reflect everything at twice its normal size and twisting every bit of advice from Reason in midair, turning it to inflammatory bile.

Assumption and Insecurity are the parents of Jealousy—and oh, what a poi-sonous pair they make! When their misbegotten, green-eyed offspring tries to turn your mind inside out, Assumption and Insecurity will spare no pains to assist their child. Difficult as it may be, you must look them all in the eye and name them for what they are. Only then will Jealousy peevishly, reluctantly relinquish its hold on your heart. Only then will Reason and Trust come to call.*

If you suspect the worst of someone else but do not know the facts, remember: when in doubt, don't assume, ask.

* With a nod to the delightful *Book of Qualities* by J. Ruth Gendler.

A Cake for Sholom and Sarah

POLAND

E very day Sholom walked down the street from his ramshackle house at the top of the hill. The men always tipped their hats and the mothers poked their children to bow or curtsey, for Sholom was the *melamed*, their teacher. And when Sarah went to the market, the women always smiled politely and the butcher gave her an extra soup bone, for she was the *melamed's* wife. They were a well-respected couple in the town of Chelm, but they never had a kopek to spare.

When Sholom went into town, his elbows poked through the sleeves of his threadbare black coat and his secondhand trousers flapped on his bony legs. When Sarah opened her cupboard doors, she saw scrawny mice scuffling over the few stale crumbs. Sholom and Sarah were so poor they never heard the sweet sound of silver jingling in their pockets.

Sholom could not understand why such an astute, clever fellow such as himself should lead such a miserable life. One day he came puffing and panting up the hill and sank onto a chair. "Why are we so poor, Sarah?" he whined. "All we ever have is gruel and cabbage. Why don't we ever have a honey cake like the one we had at the wedding of the wine merchant's daughter? I can still taste that cake. *Mmmm.*"

He closed his eyes and licked his lips and Sarah slapped him with her dishrag. "Why are we so poor? Why do you bother to ask, you *schlimazl?* Why do dogs chase cats? Some things just are the way they are. Now be quiet and eat your dinner."

But Sholom had made up his mind that they deserved a sweet—a luxury such as the rich took for granted every day—and he was determined to have it. Deep thinker that he was, this learned scholar sat in steadfast contemplation till his soup grew cold. But at last he looked up at his wife with a sly wink. Sholom checked outside to see if anyone was lurking nearby, then closed the door tightly and drew the flour sack curtains over the windows. He crooked a finger at Sarah, and she huddled close to listen as he whispered his plan to her. A smile spread across Sarah's face and she nodded eagerly as he spoke.

Sholom proposed that they could have a cake as luscious as the ones eaten by Moishe the wine merchant and his family. "It's just a matter of management, my girl," he explained to Sarah. "We must save up our money, a little at a time, each of us adding a kopek once a week, and before we know it, we'll have enough to buy the ingredients for the richest cake ever tasted in Chelm!"

Sarah clapped her hands and twirled around. Wide-eyed, she whispered to him, "Where shall we hide these kopeks, husband, so that no one will find them?"

Sholom pointed to a dilapidated wooden chest sitting near the door of their hut on four wobbly wheels. He opened its hinged lid and tossed out the moth-eaten rags and dented pots, then sealed it with a rusty padlock. With the tip of their axe he poked a small hole in the lid and then covered the hole with a scrap of cloth. Sarah giggled and hugged her cunning husband. Together they solemnly lifted a corner of the cloth, dropped their kopeks into the chest and heard the satisfying sound of the two coins clinking together.

Sholom decided that he would deposit his coin on Friday mornings when he arose. Sarah said she'd put hers in on Friday afternoons when he had gone to the synagogue. It was a brilliant plan and it worked just perfectly.

When they sat at dinner eating gritty grey kasha, they remembered their kopeks piling up in the chest and grinned and winked at one another. As Sarah passed by the shop windows full of lace-trimmed hats and velvet skirts she just tossed her head, knowing that at home their secret store of coins was growing ever larger. And when Sholom saw a prosperous townsman pulling a silver watch from his vest pocket, he would smile and nod at the man in a knowing way, confident that he, too, had wealth amassed in his very own wooden vault.

Sometimes Sarah would say, "Sholom, you're still putting in those kopeks, aren't you, my darling?" And Sholom would reply, "We'll be eating cake before you know it, my sweet."

And sometimes Sholom would say, "Sarah, I can almost taste that honey cake. You're still putting in your kopeks, aren't you, my dear?" Sarah would smile and reply, "I'm sure that chest will be full soon, Sholom."

One warm summer's day, Sholom reckoned that enough coins had accumulated to purchase the makings of the cake. Sarah waited breathlessly at his shoulder as he broke the hasp holding the lock. The lid creaked open, and they both peered in to gloat over their hoard. There at the bottom of the chest were two kopeks. Just two dull, tiny kopeks.

Sarah wailed. "Oh Sholom, we've been robbed!"

"Impossible! The chest has been locked for months! You saw me break the lock, woman!"

At the same time they turned on each other, eyes wide, nostrils flaring. "Why didn't you put your coins in as you agreed?" "Where are all of those kopeks you promised to save?" "You liar, you cheat, you perfidious wretch!"

Sholom bellowed for silence. Sarah glared spitefully as he explained that he had given the matter much thought and had come to the conclusion that he could use his kopeks to greater advantage in administering the household affairs. Furthermore, he had reasoned that Sarah, worthy housekeeper that she was, would have faithfully deposited sufficient coinage to purchase the cake ingredients. He was most grievously disappointed to find that his trust had been misplaced and that Sarah had not kept her end of the bargain. Sholom shook his fist under her nose.

Sarah was almost speechless with fury. Almost, but not quite. "*My* end of the bargain?" she shrieked. "*My* end? What of *your* promise? I thought this matter over very carefully as well. With the pitiful amount of money that you give me each month, I realized that I couldn't possibly spare even a measly kopek for your silly cake. So I, prudent housekeeper that I am, decided to save my money for chicken necks and turnips, to keep us together body and soul. I long ago calculated that your kopeks alone would buy the makings of a cake and even a bottle of schnapps to go with it, but now we have no more than we started with, and it's all your fault!"

Eyes blazing, the couple leapt at one another. They throttled and whacked and pinched and smacked. At last Sarah shoved Sholom with all her might, and he toppled over backwards into the open trunk. Sholom grabbed at Sarah as he fell, and the two of them landed in the chest. The lid slammed down on them with a thud and the chest began to move. Trapped inside, the scholar and his wife continued to pummel one another. The rickety trunk rocked back and forth, and the rusty wheels squeaked as the creaking wooden box slowly rolled out of the open door and onto the street.

The chest perched, teetering at the brow of the hill. Sarah snatched a fistful of Sholom's hair and knocked his head against one of the walls. With a shiver, the trunk sailed off down the street, wheels screeching, sparks flying, the two inside howling and screaming. The chest caught an old woman by surprise as she trudged up the hill with her basket of laundry. It knocked the basket from her hands and continued down the street with a pair of pantaloons caught on a splinter, waving like a flag.

At the bottom of the hill it plowed into a vendor's cart full of fruit. A watermelon exploded over the top of the chest and splattered through the cracked boards of the lid. Sholom and Sarah both tried to clamber out but this only caused the trunk to lurch onto two wheels and veer around a corner so that it continued to roll through the town.

All the residents of Chelm could hear the uproar, and half of them ran after the rolling chestful of demons. Dogs raced beside the chest barking and nipping at the screeching wheels, little children dared one another to whack it with sticks, and women threw their aprons over their heads in terror at its coming.

As the decrepit trunk careened down the cobblestoned streets, a woman's arm poked out of the top planking and a man's leg came through a side wall, kicking wildly. Moishe the wine merchant was just coming out of his shop and had bent over to lock his door when the renegade trunk sped by and Sholom's foot booted Moishe headfirst into the brick wall. The chest squealed along, pitching and yawling like a boat on the high seas as the two within struggled to either claw their way out or kill one another—or both.

The street began to level out as it neared the river at the edge of town, but that trunk simply streaked by the townsfolk in a blur. The bridge at the foot of the street came nearer and nearer. By this time everyone in Chelm was chasing the bedemoned trunk, hoping to push it into the water. Suddenly, one of the wheels flew off, and the chest pitched over onto its side and slid to a halt two feet from the riverbank.

An eerie silence enveloped the town of Chelm, save for a whirring noise as one wheel of the chest slowly spun to a standstill. While the astonished townspeople watched, the remains of the trunk collapsed onto Sholom, their *melamed*, and Sarah, his wife.

For a full minute nothing moved among the wreckage. Then slowly the scholar stood up and brushed wooden splinters from his beard. Sarah tottered to her feet and smoothed down her dress. The couple said nothing, just eyed one another with contempt. But as they turned to walk back to their house, they heard a faint clinking sound. Looking down, Sholom and Sarah saw two kopeks—two dull, tiny kopeks—lying together in the street.

Sarah bent to snatch them up at the same moment that Sholom reached for the coins. With a snarl and a yelp they were tangled up again, grappling on the cobblestones. Suddenly they rolled out of sight. There was a loud splash, some muffled thrashings and squawks, and then nothing but the sound of the river chuckling to itself as it flowed by.

When the good people of Chelm peered over the edge of the bank, they saw a stream of bubbles and a scrap of wood floating on the current. As for Sholom, the *melamed*, and his wife Sarah, not a trace of them was ever seen again.

Sholom and Sarah didn't need a chest stuffed with kopeks to make them happy. They needed a chest filled with hope—a hope chest.

When I was growing up, every girl wanted a hope chest. For a lucky girl's sixteenth birthday, her parents would give her a handsome wooden chest that would sit at the foot of her bed, a constant reminder of her most cherished dream. It was to be filled with linens and dishes, glassware and other household goods for a young couple's home. Really industrious girls would sew, embroider, or crochet the pillowcases and luncheon napkins themselves.

Oh, how I wish I had been given a hope chest. But instead of tea towels and tablecloths, I wish my grandmothers and aunts, godmothers and friends could have packed it with tokens of their experience, the wisdom that helped them thrive in their married lives. Hope would still have been the most important thing to go into such a chest, for without faith and optimism even the most promising relationships can founder. But there are other, equally necessary things a union needs to sustain it, qualities like trust and honesty, respect and responsibility. I wish my loved ones had shared those secrets with me.

I cannot tell you how many times Tom and I fell into a dilapidated old trunk and screeched all over town, making fools of ourselves, before it finally fell apart and we had to find a new one. (Luckily, we never fell into the river.) Through the years we've collected a trunkful of down-to-earth advice and well-tempered strategies for negotiating a partnership. I can see that there are plenty of other couples, like Sholom and Sarah, who could also use such a treasure trove.

The Selkie Wife

SCOTLAND

Once, long ago, a man named Michael lived close to the wild and wind-swept sea. He spent his days in a boat, casting his nets into the water, and he spent his nights mending those nets by the light of the fire in his hut. It was a lonely life, a hard life, and as Michael sat before the hearth, he wished he had a wife—someone to share the work with him, someone to warm his narrow bed at night.

Michael would think of this woman. In his mind he'd hear her voice, soft and sweet, he'd smell her soft, thick hair, he'd feel the touch of her hands caressing him. He dreamed of her playing with their children, planting flowers by the doorstep, having a mug of hot tea ready for him when he came in at night, chilled from a day on the water. Oh, it would be a fine life, indeed, with a woman to share it . . . but he never did more than dream. Each morning he was up before the sun, and each evening he was too tired to stir from his house. Yet still he wished for a wife of his own.

One summer, as the days grew long and the evening sky stayed bright, Michael felt a restless tide pulling at his heart. Night after night he left his hut and went back down to the sea where he walked along the shore, sighing and tossing bits of shell into the waves. There was a presence in the air—he could almost smell it—and it told him that something was about to happen.

Michael would walk till he judged it was close to midnight and all he ever saw was the sand, strewn with rock, stinking of fish and bracken. At last he would shake himself. "I will never be up again for the fishing if I don't get back now." Then he would trudge home, weary and bemused.

But one night, as he turned to go, the wind at his back changed. It seemed to carry a bit of weird music, a song that tickled his ear and made him stop and look around. There, a few yards off shore, he saw a cropping of black rock, washed slick by the waves. And there on the rocks were three seals. It seemed to him that the singing was coming from them.

One by one, the seals pulled themselves up onto their hind flippers, raised their snouts to the sky and shook their heads. Then their dark, glistening fur skins slowly slipped from their bodies, and standing on the rock were three beautiful women—selkies. The young women did not see Michael. They stretched their pale arms and legs and tossed their long, black hair over their shoulders. Then, laughing and calling to one another, they dove into the waves.

Michael gasped, not believing his own eyes. Then he smiled. He sank to the sand and watched the women as they played in the water, sat on the rocks, combed each other's hair, and sang their eerie, wordless tunes. As Michael stared at the three selkies, his gaze was drawn again and again to the smallest and loveliest one. Flushed with desire, he began to plot how to capture the beautiful creature and make her his own.

Everyone who lives beside the sea has heard tales of the selkies, the seal people. It is said that they came ashore once a year, on Midsummer's Eve. In some villages, good luck in a fishing family is said to come from selkie blood, from one who had left the water and married a human man or woman. And there are other tales, of fishermen who stole a seal's skin and then could ask whatever they wished of the selkie.

Michael made up his mind to take the selkie maiden's skin when he got the chance. But while he crouched, ready to slip into the water as soon as the women were out of sight, they climbed onto the rocks once more, picked up their pelts, and pulled the fur up over their bodies. Michael moaned with disappointment as the three seals slid into the water and vanished into the waves.

From that night forth, Michael thought of nothing else but the selkie maid. The passing of time had never mattered much to Michael before, but after seeing the young seal woman, the turning of the seasons were a torment to him. The rest of the summer and autumn passed in a haze. Never had the winter nights seemed so endless, the spring sun so slow in quickening the wild bluebells to bloom.

At last, at last, summer was upon him again. Every day his pulse raced as he hauled his boat ashore, cleaned his catch, and went to town to sell his fish. When Michael returned in the early evening, he gulped a meal and then set off for the seal maidens' rocks.

There he sat, still as a rock himself, scarcely breathing. His eyes ached as he watched for a sign of his selkie lass. In his mind he had lived with her for a year already and so he thought of her as his own fair love—as if it were truly so.

Night after night, Michael dragged himself away, disappointed and forlorn. He began to fret that he had missed them or that they had gone to a different place. Sometimes he wondered if he had ever seen them at all or whether they were just the fevered dream of a fool.

It seemed to him that high summer had long since come and gone. One day he mentioned this to the fish merchant in town and the man laughed.

"Is it midsummer you're pining for, man? Well, this is it, the very day. And there's many a lass in town here who wouldn't frown at dancin' round the bonfire with ye this evening, Michael."

Michael collected his money and ran nearly all the way home. He was too excited to eat at all. He hurried down the beach until he came to the selkie rocks and then sat and waited under a pale, silvery sky for the seals to return.

And they came. Yes, just as he had dreamed so many, many times, their sleek, dark heads came bobbing up out of the waves. The young man watched, breathless, as they clambered onto the rocks and drew themselves up. He shuddered as, one by one, they shed their fur pelts and stretched their arms and legs before they laughed and plunged back into the waves.

Michael did not hesitate. As soon as they swam off out of sight, he threw himself into the water and made for the black rocks. He picked up the selkie skin. It was still warm from her body. In great haste, he rolled up the pelt and tucked it inside his shirt, then he slipped soundlessly into the sea, swam back to shore, and ran off.

Her cries reached him far down the beach, stopped him shivering in his tracks.

They would have rent the heart of a less determined man. But his longing was greater than his pity, and he smiled at the success of his plan.

He hid the seal skin in the loft of his shed, and in the morning Michael returned to the cropping of rocks. The selkie maid sat weeping on the shore. She started in alarm at the sight of a human, but he was gentle. He wrapped her in a blanket and spoke soothingly to her, though she could not understand his words. Michael carried her most of the way to his hut, for the coarse sand hurt her tender feet. His heart thudded against his chest so hard he thought surely she could hear it.

So that is how Michael caught the selkie woman and made her his wife. They lived together beside the sea and she bore him seven children. She spoke little and rarely smiled, but she was a good mother and a hard worker, and she warmed his bed at night.

Heeding the tales he'd heard, Michael was careful to keep the seal skin well hidden. Once a year, he'd go into his shed and close the door behind him. Then he'd take down from the loft a small bundle and unwrap it. For a time he would hold in his hands his dear wife's skin, the fur pelt she'd worn before she came to live with him. He would oil the skin to keep it supple and brush the fur to keep it shiny. And then the skin would be rolled up tight and tucked away in the farthest corner of the loft for another year.

Whenever he oiled the seal skin, his family was sent off to the village for the day. But one year, his youngest child fell ill and Michael said he would watch the little girl while his wife and children were gone. In the afternoon, while his daughter was dozing in her cot, Michael slipped out to the shed, climbed the loft, and brought down the pelt. He left the door ajar to listen for the girl should she wake, for he was a good father and loved his children well.

Carefully he unwrapped the bundle and laid it on his knees. He stroked the soft, dark fur, now beginning to grey, and smiled fondly as he remembered the night he'd first seen his lovely selkie bride. He oiled the skin and brushed it, then wrapped it up once more. And Michael never saw his little daughter, solemn and silent like her mother, come quietly to the door and peek in, then just as quietly go away, back to her bed.

The next morning Michael was out on the water casting his deep nets. The sun was well up in the sky before he felt the wind change. It was carrying a song, a wordless melody that chilled him like a winter's gale. His heart was sick with foreknowing as he clawed at the nets. Ever since the selkie had lived with him, his nets had always been full. This day was no different; he strained at the heavy catch. The song rose to a shrilling wail as he struggled to bring the haul on board, and Michael went mad with fear. He drew out his knife and cut the cords, slicing through his best nets to be free of the weight. Then he rowed for shore.

He skidded the boat halfway out of the water and leaped to the sand. He sprinted up the beach toward his house and saw his children standing at the water's edge, weeping and looking out to sea.

"Where is she?" he cried, and without a word they pointed to the grey-green waves. Michael sank to his knees, sobbing, and the children gathered around him, their faces stained with tears.

"What happened?" he asked at last. The eldest told him how they were all eating their porridge when the littlest girl told their mother what she'd seen the day before: their father rubbing and brushing a dark fur skin in the shed. Then he told Michael how she had dropped the dish she was holding and it broke all to bits on the floor and she never even noticed, but her eyes had gone all shiny and dark.

And then he told how she lifted up her skirts and ran out of the house—"Yes, really, Da, she ran, Mama ran; I didn't know she could run, and then she came out of the shed with something in her hands and she was crying and laughing and looking all strange-like and she wouldn't answer us when we called to her and then she just took off. Took off runnin' to the beach and by the time we got here, she had kicked off her clothes and was pulling up that skin around her throat."

Then the youngest daughter cried out, "And then she was a seal, Da, not our mother anymore but a seal, and she went off into the water and she hasn't come back. When will Mama come back?"

Now they say that, after a time, Michael made new nets and went back to fishing, and his nets were ever full. And they say that a dark seal, a little grey in places, was often seen in the water beside Michael's boat, with her eyes big and shining and sad. But those children, they never saw their mother again, and Michael, he stayed inside on high summer evenings and never went near the seal rocks again for the rest of his days.

And that is how Michael found his selkie wife, and lost her to the wild and windswept sea.

Desire for something does not give us the right to possess it.

It took me a while to realize that I hadn't fallen in love with Tom simply for the lovely, poetic, romantic reasons I thought. The uncompromising truth is that most of us enter into our relationships out of self interest. Along with the noble and selfless reasons, we decide to join with our partners because we believe it will benefit us in a number of ways. With this in mind, the success of our unions will depend on how willing we are to understand and honor our partners' individuality. Our success will also depend on how well we can integrate our own needs and wants with those of another human being with whom we are intimately connected. That can be a lifetime's worth of work right there!

Empathy is the ability to imagine yourself in another's place and then act out of respect based on that knowledge. Empathy is not a subject that is taught in our schools. It is not often modeled in our homes. As a society, we do not value empathy overmuch. It is easy to assume that you know all about your dearest heart, but are you certain that you know what your lover really wants? How your lover really feels? Though the answers may surprise or unsettle you, it is important for both of you to know these truths about one another—and then, to act accordingly.

Who Should Close the Door?

INDIA

Long ago, but perhaps not so long as you might think, and far away, but certainly closer than you would guess, there lived a couple. A very stubborn couple. In fact, since people first began living together, there has never been, and likely there will never be, two people more stubborn than Radha and Gopal.

They spent most of their time quarreling, contradicting one another, and plotting ways to prove the other wrong. The rest of their time they spent sulking, denying accusations, and refusing to admit that they ever made mistakes. Their neighbors learned to turn a deaf ear to their screamed threats and barbed insults. They also learned to keep a wary eye out for tossed pots and hurled sticks of bamboo flying through the windows.

And yet, if you were to ask Radha or Gopal if they were happy with their marriage, if they loved one another, they would say "yes." Despite their roaring and ruckus (or perhaps, just perhaps, *because* of it), they really were quite fond of each other . . . sometimes. Radha was certain that Sita would shower them with never-ending bliss just as soon as Gopal finally gave in and did whatever she commanded—er, suggested. And Gopal was equally convinced that all would be well as soon as Radha admitted that *he* was as clear-headed and wise as Rama himself. Believe me, this kept the neighbors confused! One minute they'd see Radha with her arms around Gopal's neck, kissing him affectionately. Two minutes later, they'd see a pile of his clothes sailing out the door and Gopal tumbling out behind them.

Can you imagine such a couple? Aren't you glad you don't know anyone like them?

Now one day Radha and Gopal were eating their afternoon meal when the door of their hut blew open. In some households, whoever was nearest the door would simply get up and shut it, without a word said. In other households, the youngest child able to walk would be asked to get up and shut the door. But in Radha and Gopal's household, this was a moment ripe for discord and disaster.

"Radha, the door has blown open. Go close it," Gopal said, with his mouth full of rice.

"Why should *I* close the door?" she retorted. "*You* thought of it. *You* close it."

"Because I am eating, woman," Gopal explained with exaggerated patience. "Now get up and close the door."

Radha was already fuming. "*You* are eating. *You* are eating! Just what do you think *I* am doing, eh? I am *serving* you. But do you care about me? *Hmmph.* No. I will not get up and close the door. *You* are closer; you do it, you big, selfish ox."

With great effort, Gopal managed to control himself, although he was outraged at Radha's insult. "Now Radha, you know that name-calling is not a proper way to speak to one another. Just for that, *you* must get up and close the door!"

First Radha deftly absolved herself of any necessity to apologize to Gopal. "I most certainly will not! I wasn't name-calling, I was only telling the truth—you *are* a big, selfish ox." Then she displayed her shrewd, logical mind. "Besides, you built that miserable, flimsy, little bundle of rotting reeds that you call a door, so it is your door. It is only fitting that you should take care of what is yours. Go shut the door, Gopal."

Gopal almost choked on his rice. His face turned red, his eyes bulged, he heaved up off of the floor. He shook his finger in Radha's face and threatened her with the loss of her front teeth, rearrangement of her facial features, and permanent hair removal.

Radha glared back at him and sneered at his threats. Soon dishes were flying across the room and jars were crashing on the floor. Shrieks and snarls shook the roof poles. And then suddenly the noise stopped. There was an unsettling quiet in the hut, and the neighbors peeked through their windows to see if perhaps, at long last, harmony's darlings had accidentally killed one another.

Standing amidst the ruins of the house were Gopal and Radha, breathing hard, toe to toe, nose to nose, fists clenched at their sides. Then they heard Radha hiss, "I have an idea. Whoever speaks first, from this moment on, will have to close the door. Agreed?"

Gopal chewed his lip and narrowed one eye suspiciously; the effort of analyzing this suggestion, hunting for hidden traps or unfair advantages to Radha, was obvious on his face. After several minutes, he nodded. "Agreed."

And so the two of them sat down on opposite ends of the *charpai*, crossed their arms over their chests, and stewed—silently.

Can you imagine such a couple? Aren't you glad you don't know anyone like them?

Radha and Gopal sat on the bed like that for a short time, but with the door hanging open it wasn't long before a quivering, curious nose poked its way around the doorframe. A hungry stray dog stepped cautiously into the house and looked at the two humans. They watched her, too, but neither one raised a hand or shouted for her to leave. She could sense their anger, but since they sat still as stones, after a bit she slinked into the room and gobbled up the spilled rice and *dal.*

Helpless, Radha and Gopal watched as the dog became bolder and sniffed about in baskets, pushed over jars, lapped up *ghee,* and ate a stack of fresh *chapattis.* When she was full she trotted toward the door, tail held high, and paused to lick a streak of lentil sauce off of Gopal's hand. Gopal breathed hard but said not a word as the dog left the hut.

Later, one of the villagers came walking by and glanced in on the stolid, sulking couple. He called out a greeting but they did not answer him. They did not move or respond to anything he said. As the fellow grasped the situation, he chuckled to himself.

"Either they're deaf and dumb or under a spell. Whatever has happened here, I'm sure Radha and Gopal won't mind if I, *ahem,* borrow a few things," he muttered. Husband and wife stared in disbelief as the man poked around among their tools. He stuffed a hoe, an axe, and a coil of rope into a sack. When they remained silent and made no effort to stop him, the fellow picked up a *sari* and a pair of pajamas as well. Then he thanked them politely and left, stifling a smile at the sight of their flushed, scowling faces.

Night fell and the neighbors were incredulous. They had not had such uninter-rupted peace and quiet in years! As the moon rose and shone into the cluttered, silent house, Radha and Gopal still sat on their bed, angrier than ever at each other for allowing the dog and the man to take their food and belongings.

Under cover of darkness, a thief came creeping into the village. Up and down the streets he slipped, from shadow to shadow, until he spied an unlit hut with the door wide open. He watched, hidden, as the neighbors called to the folks within. He noted how some of them went into the house empty-handed yet emerged with a bowl or a mat or some other small thing in their hands. Slowly, soundlessly, he edged around the corner and into the disheveled house. There he saw a man and woman, seated on a *charpai*, looking at him without a word. The thief began to smile; this was his lucky night.

He picked his way carefully through the litter of scattered beans, broken cups, and tangled rugs. With an instinct born of years of practice at his dubious craft, the thief went straight to the wooden box where Radha and Gopal had hidden their modest store of coins. He kept his eyes on them as he deftly picked the lock and opened the box. They both turned livid, shaking with fury, but the thief was greatly amused to see that they still remained speechless. He scooped out the *rupees*, every single bit of the couple's treasure, and crammed them into his pockets. Then he stepped lightly across the room and tweaked Gopal's nose.

"You know, you really ought to think of a more clever spot to hide your money next time. Such a simpleton."

Gopal lunged off of the *charpai*. "It wasn't me who put it there!" he bellowed. "*She* did it! She's your fool!" He pointed to his wife.

The thief ducked past Radha, his pockets jangling with their savings, but she ignored him. Instead, she jumped up from the bed and whirled on her husband. Gloating in triumph, Radha crowed, "Ha! You spoke first, you fool. And now, Gopal, *you* must shut the door!"

Can you imagine such a couple? Aren't you glad you don't know anyone like them?

If you occasionally quarrel with your partner, take heart: everyone succumbs to fits of anger or hurt feelings at times. For a couple of years I had the regrettable habit of bringing up a problem just before we went to sleep. Those late-night wrangles were a one-way ticket to trouble; they never seemed to resolve themselves amicably, but I was too stubborn to restrain myself. Finally, I decided to forgo my Nana's one piece of marital advice: "Never go to bed angry with each other." Instead, I recalled a passage from a Russian folktale, "Vasilisa the Beautiful," which my friend Carolyn shared with me:

As young Vasilisa's mother lay on her deathbed, she gave her daughter a small doll and advised her to confide in the doll and tell it all of her troubles. She assured Vasilisa that the doll would take care of her. True enough, when the young girl was in dire distress and poured her heart out to the little figure, the doll guided and consoled her. She always ended her counsel with the reminder, "Morning is better than evening, Vasilisa, morning is better than evening."

I remembered that little mantra when we got into our bedtime "discussions," and I stopped trying to dissolve every particle of our disagreement before we slept. And truly, morning was better when it came to resolving conflicts, because we'd both had a chance to fly away from the scene of the disaster while we slept. Mighty chasms in our relationship shrank back down to the minor fissures they really were. Our pride and stubbornness seemed to evaporate overnight and we awoke able to talk about our differences calmly. To tell you the truth, at this point I cannot even remember the last time we had a fight before bed.

Don't you wish your union were blessed with a little doll for each of you to slip into your pockets and pull out when you were at your wits' end? Maybe you and your sweetie could set a date to make a couple of those little figures for yourselves. Taking the time to fashion that wise, guiding energy into a physical form could be very helpful the next time you are overwhelmed by anger, pride—or plain old idiocy.

The Wife Who Would Not Be Pleased

FINLAND

Once upon a time there was a woman who was so wayward, so fractious, so rilesome, so intractable, so, so . . . well, let me just tell you about her and you can see for yourself what I mean.

Helmi was such a pretty young thing, Timo thought she would make a good wife. Now isn't that always the way these things begin? You see a handsome fellow or a beautiful girl, and all your sense goes out the window! And no one in love ever believes a word against his sweetheart, especially when it is true.

Oh dear, why didn't he listen? His mother tried to tell him, his sister tried to tell him, all of his friends *did* tell him, but did Timo listen? No. No, no, no, no, *no*. He was in love!

So, after the harvest Timo married pretty Helmi—and believe me, it was a lovely wedding. But even before the marriage feast was over, Timo began to see that Helmi's temperament was not as beguiling as her looks. Why, she was so perverse, she would disagree with him even when she knew he was right!

Now Timo was an obliging sort of fellow, and at first he tried to please her so that she wasn't so cross and sulky. He brought her a shiny new pot all the way from Espoo, but she pointed out that he could have gotten a better deal in Turku, and besides, she wanted a pan, not a pot. He kept trying, bless his heart, but you and I know that there is nothing in the world that will satisfy a woman who doesn't want to be pleased. And Helmi didn't want to be pleased. She just wanted to be *right*. When she could be right, aaah, then she was as happy as a bear in a thimbleberry patch!

Before they'd been married a month, Timo decided that if Helmi wanted to be right, well then, he'd let her be right. It was much easier that way. She would say,

"The geese are molting, I'd better gather up their feathers so I can stuff pillows." Even though he had just fed the geese and knew they hadn't dropped so much as a pinfeather, he would agree with her. Then he could go off and sharpen his sickle or mend a rake or oil a harness in peace.

Alas, this only worked for awhile, because Helmi would pout if she didn't have at least one good, rousing argument every day. Timo tried sleeping later or working longer, but eventually he had to get out of bed or come in from the fields or sit down to supper, and then all of her grumbling bubbled over and scalded him like hot milk splattering a stove.

When the snows began to fall there was no getting away from her. They sat in the sauna and when he splashed water on the rocks, she said that it was too soon and he'd crack them. If he waited, then she said that it was too late and she was baked to a crisp. Either way she beat him with the birch twigs till he yelped.

So they bumbled along like this, with Helmi trying to rile him to take a stand on the likelihood of the Northern Lights shining on a Thursday, the best way to treat the dog's fleas, or how long it should take to ski into town in five feet of snow—and with Timo doing his best to dodge Helmi's sharp tongue.

One day in early summer they went tramping into the village for supplies. And what do you know, they were arguing! Well, not really, for Helmi was doing a fine job of holding up both ends of the conversation all by herself. Timo was doing his best to placate her, mostly by keeping silent.

She was wondering what he would do if she died. "Of course," Helmi sniffed, "if you *really* loved me, you would never even look at another woman, but I'll bet you would get married again before I was even cold in the ground." She became sullen when he did not answer and took his silence for an admission of guilt—yes, he *would* marry another woman if she should die! Helmi berated him for not loving her, for wanting to marry another woman, for wishing that she were dead!

They came to a weathered bridge across a swollen river. The bridge shuddered and shook under the onslaught of the snowmelt. Helmi's accusations rose to a crescendo as they reached the middle of the span, and Timo turned around to face her. The river was roaring and she could see her husband moving his lips but she could not hear his words. Beside herself with rage, she began jumping up and down.

Timo was alarmed to see the old planks buckling and cracking under her weight. He pointed down and called out to warn her, but Helmi just tossed her head. "I'll show *you!*" she screamed and jumped all the harder. The boards split apart and down she went, straight into the water below, where she was swept under by the strong current.

Timo stood stock still for a moment, thunderstruck. Then he gathered his wits about him and began running along the riverbank. He called to two men lashing logs together. "Have you seen my wife? She fell into the river!"

"Where did she fall in?"

"Back there, the bridge gave way under her."

"Then get downstream, the way the water flows, you fool, and look for her!"

Timo shook his head. "Oh no, you don't know my wife! She'll be up *here!*"

"You're crazy, man. No one could swim against that current. It would drown an ox."

"You really don't know my wife."

Timo grabbed a fallen branch, crouched at the water's edge, and stared at the rushing river. Several long minutes passed. The two woodsmen rubbed their chins and looked at him, then at the water, and back at him again.

Suddenly, they saw a spot of red kerchief and a yellow braid go bobbing along, headed upstream. Timo pointed.

"There now, my friends, I told you so. There is my wife!"

The three men held onto the branch and tried to snag Helmi as she swirled by, but whenever it seemed that they had caught her, the sodden mass twisted out of their reach.

After Helmi disappeared around a bend in the river, the other men turned to Timo, shaking their heads in disbelief. "She must have been as stubborn as a goat."

The young man looked at them and sighed. "Aye, that she was. But I'll miss her. I reckon you can get used to anything if you set your mind to it."

And you know what? Timo was right.

Everyone likes to be right. I certainly do. But being right starts to lose its allure after awhile. For a moment I am transported to the top of the Mountain of Self-Righteousness, where I feel smug and elated. Then, after about five minutes, I begin to notice just how far from Tom I am. I see that the footbridge across the gorge has been washed away, and it starts to feel a bit windy and desolate—and boring. I try my best to continue gloating over my victory, but in the long run I would rather be reconciled than right, so I climb down off the mountain (which usually results in some tender, bruised spots) and we make amends.

Learning how to negotiate, how to discuss and compromise, is a fine art. Some people get paid a lot of money to do such a thing! In a relationship, it takes courage and determination to master this skill. Figuring out a better way to make your point than just proving that you're right requires divine wisdom. Sometimes, divine wisdom is figuring out that you don't have to make your point at all.

Perhaps all couples should heed the wisdom of the Chinese to ensure domestic tranquility: we should plant a pair of Nandina domestica bushes outside our back doors. In China, these beautiful, red berried shrubs are planted beside the doors of a newly wedded couple's home. Whenever the bride or groom is troubled by a marital dispute, they go out and make their complaints to their bush. It absorbs all the upset, and the spouse returns to their partner with a clear heart and mind. The common name for this therapeutic plant wonder is "heavenly bamboo"; I think it should be included in every couple's wedding registry!

The Love Potion
KOREA

Do you know what it is like to send your beloved husband off to battle and then have him return, no longer the man you once loved? It happened to Yun Ok, and this is what she did to bring him back home again, body and soul, heart and mind.

⟨⟨⟩⟩

Many, many years ago, a young farmer went away to fight in a war. His wife, Yun Ok, stayed behind on their farm, worrying and waiting, praying for his safe return. When he came back, Yun Ok rejoiced. She cooked lavish meals of his favorite foods. She showed him their plump chickens, the trees burdened with ripe plums, and the sacks of rice and crocks of *kimchi* she had stored. But though his body was as strong and firm as before, his spirit was deeply scarred.

He pushed aside the food she served, he made no move to harvest the fruit, he walked through their fields with unseeing eyes, arms limp at his sides. Her kind, gentle husband spoke sharply to her and would not answer her questions. When they lay together at night, he never touched her.

Yun Ok shook her head, bit her lip, and dared to do things no good wife should do. She spent some of their precious silver to purchase persimmons and sesame sweets to tempt him. She pushed a hoe into his hands, waved to him from the fields to come help with the cutting, and begged him to fill baskets with rice after the threshing. She perfumed her hair and took her silk wedding dress from the chest in the loft, and then Yun Ok offered him all the love she had faithfully kept for the long years they had been parted.

Days, then weeks passed, but Yun Ok's husband did not change. Despite her proddings, he would not speak of what he had seen and done; he only grew more surly and distant. In despair, Yun Ok admitted to herself that his heart no longer belonged to her.

In those days an old *mudang*, a shaman, lived in the mountains a day's walk to the west. She was both feared and respected for her magical powers, and Yun Ok decided to seek her counsel.

At dawn one morning she told her husband, "I am going on a journey."

He did not reply.

"I will be gone two days. I have left rice and fish and squash for you."

Silence.

"I will miss you."

No answer.

Yun Ok sighed, shouldered her pouch, and left her husband staring into the fire. She traveled through steep, rocky country and spent the night on the mountainside. In the morning she approached the hermit's cave and found the old woman sunning herself. Yun Ok knelt and bowed before her.

"Most wise and honored Grandmother, my husband is in need of healing. Since he has come back from the war, he is a stranger in my arms." Then she began to cry, telling the shaman all she had done to win him back, to cheer him and please him again. She told of his cross temper or cold indifference to everything she did. She begged the old shaman to help her.

The shaman was, truly, a very wise woman. As to whether she had magical powers, well, she *could* sometimes produce the miraculous from the impossible, but only with the aid of willing hands and trusting hearts. She listened to the young wife's brokenhearted tale impassively, then agreed to help her on one condition.

"You must bring me a fresh whisker from the tiger that lives in the hills beyond your village."

Yun Ok gasped. "A tiger's *whisker?* But Grandmother, I cannot . . . I mean, how could I . . . it is impossible to approach a live tiger—"

The *mudang* spoke brusquely. "If you wish to win your husband's heart again, you will find a way. I have nothing more to say."

Yun Ok had expected to receive a pungent-smelling powder that she would stir into his food, or a complicated spell to chant over her husband while he was sleeping —never a task that would put her life in peril.

All the way home she thought of how she might accomplish such a thing. Perhaps she could pay the bravest hunter in the village to slay the tiger and bring her its whiskers. Perhaps she could lure the tiger into a trap she built and pull one of his whiskers out while he was penned up and could not move. It even crossed her mind that perhaps she might trick the shaman with a whisker from some other creature. After all, how many people have ever seen a fresh tiger's whisker?

But in her heart, Yun Ok knew that there was really only one way to fulfill the *mudang's* request. She alone would have to seek out the creature in his lair and pluck one of the whiskers from that tiger herself, without harming him in any way.

The very next night, as her husband slept, Yun Ok crept from her hut with a bowl of rice and chicken broth. The young woman wandered up into the hills till she heard the tiger roaring far off. She dropped the bowl in terror and ran back to her farm. This happened again and again, for many nights.

But Yun Ok's husband grew no kinder, no happier. So once more she set out with food for the tiger. She had asked the hunters in the village where she could find the tiger's den, and she made her way toward it with a pounding heart and unsteady footsteps. Every snapping twig froze her in her tracks. When the great animal roared nearby, she forced herself not to scream or panic. She set the fresh meat on the ground and backed away down the trail.

Each night she ventured further into the forest, walking cautiously toward the tiger's lair till at last she found it. There she watched and listened for signs of the animal, but he was gone. She left the meat some distance from the rocky entrance to his cave, then raced back to her home.

After a time, she became braver. Some nights he was off hunting in the hills and she could leave the meat a bit closer to the den. Other nights she could hear him crunching the bones of his meal, and Yun Ok paused only a moment before she placed the food on the path and left.

Then one night when the moon was full, Yun Ok met the tiger as he was returning with his kill. His belly bulged and the rest of the carcass hung from his mouth. He stopped, golden eyes glittering and tail sweeping back and forth lazily on the ground. Yun Ok did not flee. She bowed and placed a chunk of raw fish on the ground. "Mighty one, I bring you food in peace. I have brought food to you many times. I go in peace. I'll come again tomorrow."

The tiger did not move as she backed away. When he did not follow, she turned and ran headlong through the trees until she found a trail out of the hills.

It took much courage to walk into those hills the next night. But Yun Ok prayed that the tiger would recognize her scent and remember that she brought meat for him. As she approached the den, she heard the tiger snoring. She set down half a chicken close to the mouth of the cave and then crouched in the darkness, waiting for the moon to rise.

When the tiger came out of his lair, he sniffed the air and turned to the woman. Yun Ok held her breath. He twitched his tail once, then bent over the meat and began to eat.

In the nights that followed, Yun Ok brought food to the tiger's den and then squatted nearby as he ate it. Sometimes she spoke quietly. When the tiger finished eating he washed himself, then laid on his side with his eyes half closed, purring. Yun Ok chuckled softly to herself.

Once more the moon rose full, and Yun Ok joined the tiger for his evening meal. As he lay there purring afterward, she knelt beside the enormous creature. She stretched out a trembling hand and, not daring to breathe, touched his huge tawny head. The tiger's purr rumbled louder as he rubbed himself against her hand.

Yun Ok sent grateful prayers flying to the spirits of the moon above, the surrounding hills, and the great beast before her. Then she scratched him behind his ears. She stroked and petted his soft coat for a long time.

"Tonight, Old Mountain Uncle, this is the night I have told you about. Tonight I am going to pull out one of your whiskers. It may hurt, just a little. I am sorry if it does, but I have told you, it is to help my dear husband. You understand, don't you?"

The tiger just pushed his massive head against her hand and rumbled deep in his throat.

With her heart pounding madly, Yun Ok reached over and grasped one of the stiff, white bristles. She muttered a quick prayer and then tugged. The whisker popped out, as long as her hand, and the tiger jerked his head in surprise. He opened his mouth wide, exposing long, sharp teeth—and then yawned. Yun Ok knelt, motionless, until he relaxed and leaned his head against her leg again.

The young woman stroked the tiger for a long time, till his purring ceased and he began to snore. Then she slowly rose and walked away down the faint track, back to her home and her husband.

Two days later, Yun Ok returned to the shaman's cave. The sharp, rocky trail blurred beneath her hurrying feet as she was swept along on a wave of wild hope. When she reached the old woman, she knelt and touched the hem of the *mudang*'s skirt in reverence. With great pride, she held out the tiger's whisker in both hands. The old woman took it without a word and scrutinized it closely, then tossed the whisker into the open fire. Yun Ok cried out and tried to snatch the hair from the flames, but it was gone.

"Oh, most wise and honored Grandmother!" she wailed. "It took months for me to get that whisker. Now how will you heal my husband?"

The shaman looked at Yun Ok sharply. "Did I ever say I would do such a thing?"

Yun Ok looked at her, puzzled, but before she could speak, the woman continued. "Dear daughter, please tell me how you, a small, helpless woman, managed to take a whisker from one of the fiercest creatures in our land. I am very curious."

And so the young wife told the *mudang* all she had done. "It took a long, long time. At first I was terrified and I didn't even know where to look for that tiger. Every time I heard him roar, no matter how far away he was, I ran. I broke many bowls that way. But then I learned where he lived and so I began to walk a little closer to the cave every night. When I found it, I didn't get too near. I just watched and waited and kept leaving food for him.

"Then one night I met him on the trail. Oh, I thought I would die of fright, Grandmother, but nothing happened! He didn't attack me—and I didn't run away. I bowed to him and left the meat.

"After that, I came up to his den every night and watched him while he ate. He got used to me. He would even lie down and purr while I was there. So I knew it was time to pluck the whisker. I talked quietly and petted him, and it just popped right into my hand."

The shaman smiled. "Dear child, you have tamed a wild, flesh-eating tiger with patience, kindness, and courage. Do you think you need more than that to heal your husband? Is it magic you want? You possess more than enough."

The old *mudang* placed her hand on Yun Ok's head and then bowed respectfully to her. Yun Ok walked home slowly, smiling to herself, thinking of the magic of a woman's love—and a tiger's whisker.

I am a great believer in magic. When I read this story for the first time many years ago, I could hardly wait to find out what remarkable spell or potion the sage would concoct with the whisker. I was pleasantly shocked when I read the end of the tale and understood the wise one's message.

One of the greatest lessons to be learned about relationships is this: there is no magical "happily ever after." The rings you exchange are not magic tokens that you merely turn three times when you want something to change. The vows and promises you will make to one another are not words of enchantment that will protect you forever and ever from all discord and disappointment. And, difficult as it may be to believe, the feelings of love that first engulf you are not proof of a spell that will remain unbroken till the end of time.

The magic that is possible in relationships happens in your own transformation. When you practice those time-honored behaviors like cultivating patience, showing respect, and practicing forgiveness, you will nourish and heal more than your relationship. I know that some of these skills are not easy to master, and they may not even be acknowledged all of the time by your partner, but trust me, eventually they do work . . . like magic.

The Sweetest Thing in the World

CZECHOSLOVAKIA

There was once a young woman who was so clever that everyone called her Clever Manka. Whenever her neighbors had a thorny problem they could not figure out, they would make their way to her little hut at the edge of the village. A man would stand there at Manka's doorstep, scratching his head, or a woman would sit down beside her, twisting her apron and frowning, and they would tell their troubles to Clever Manka. Very soon they would go away smiling, for her advice was always kind and just and, well, *clever*. Word of her cleverness spread far and wide; it even reached the palace of the king.

Now the king had not yet taken a wife, though many princesses and noblemen's daughters had been offered to him. Despite himself, he found that he was intrigued by the stories of this peasant woman. He decided that it could do no harm to meet her, and besides, he wanted to see if these tales were true. He would test Clever Manka to see just how clever she was.

So one of the king's officers rode off to Manka's village with a royal command—and a royal riddle for Manka to solve. Everyone ran from their homes or came in from the fields when the king's soldier came prancing into the village square on his strapping bay charger. He called for Clever Manka, "by order of the king," and all the neighbors whispered, wide-eyed, as a boy was sent to bring Manka in from her barley field.

When Manka arrived, the officer looked down his nose at the round-faced young woman, flushed and panting, with two thick brown braids hanging on her shoulders.

"His Majesty the King bids you to appear at his court in three days' time. He requests that you come riding, but not riding, clothed, but not clothed, and bearing a gift, but no gift." Then the officer wheeled his horse around and galloped out of the village.

When the dust had settled, Manka's neighbors clustered around her, fussing and muttering and shaking their heads. They asked her questions, warned her not to go, and stated their opinions about the wits of their ruler. But Manka assured them that all would be well. She herself was looking forward to meeting the man who had sent her such an interesting riddle to solve.

She asked one neighbor to lend her his fishing net and another for a pair of white pigeons. She put a makeshift saddle on her sturdiest nanny goat, wrapped herself up in the net, and put the birds in a covered wicker basket. Then she set off, straddling the goat with her feet dragging on the ground.

In three days' time, Manka arrived at the palace. Boldly she rode the goat straight up a long flight of polished stone stairs and into the king's royal chamber. Courtiers and soldiers, ministers and noblewomen stared, speechless, as Manka approached the throne. She dismounted, curtsied (which was rather difficult to do wrapped from neck to toe in fishing net), and then spoke.

"Your Majesty, I am Manka, from the village of Sebanov. I have come as you commanded me, riding, but not riding, clothed, but not clothed. And I have brought you a gift. Please open it."

The king took the basket and opened the lid. The two pigeons fluttered out, circled round the room several times, then flew out through an open window, heading home to their roost.

The king burst out laughing. Manka smiled as well, and the young ruler saw that she had deep dimples and flashing dark eyes. The king was delighted with Manka's cleverness, but he was eager for his ministers and advisors to recognize her keen mind as well. He posed three questions to the court and the young woman from Sebanov.

"Tell me, what is the swiftest thing in the world? What is the richest thing in the world? And what is the sweetest thing in the world?"

The courtiers and soldiers, ministers and noblewomen muttered among themselves for a long time. Manka busied herself with a bundle of clothes she had brought, shedding the net from beneath her cloak and then drawing on her skirt and blouse. At last, the prime minister stepped forth, cleared his throat, and spoke.

"Your Majesty, we have pondered these questions of yours, and we believe we know the correct answers. The swiftest thing in the world, without doubt, would be Your Highness's black stallion. The richest thing in the world would be your royal treasury, for you are the mightiest ruler of all. And the sweetest thing, Your Grace, would be the honey from your beehives, for they feed on the nectar of the apple blossoms in your orchards."

The king nodded to his prime minister. Then he turned to Manka. "Do you agree, fair Manka?"

Manka spoke carefully. "Those are thoughtful and pleasing answers, Your Majesty, but I am not certain they are the answers you were seeking." Then she smiled, and her dimples deepened. "The swiftest thing in the world is thought, Your Highness, for it can encompass a multitude of things in a moment's time. The richest thing in the world, surely, is our good Mother Earth herself, for she provides all of the riches we enjoy. And the sweetest thing in the world, my king, is love, for it heals the sick, comforts the lonely, and gladdens the hearts of all—the mightiest monarch or the simplest village maid."

Well, strange as it may seem, wit and intelligence are as strong a love potion for some as a handsome face or a comely form are to others. So it was with the king and Manka. Before those pigeons were back in Sebanov, they had fallen in love. And before the sun had set, they were married.

The king, however, set one condition on their union. "Manka, you must promise me that you will never use your cleverness to meddle in my affairs. After all, *I* am the king." Manka smiled, her dark eyes flashed, and she agreed.

Manka and her husband were very happy together for awhile. The King reveled in surprising her with gifts—garnets as large as hens' eggs, a dress of golden cloth, a fine mare as white as milk. Then, one day, two men came to petition the king for judgment in a question of ownership.

One had a mare that had given birth while they were in the great city marketplace. As the man was busy selling his wares, the newborn foal had wobbled away from its dam and tumbled under a wagon where a farmer, who owned the wagon, had found it and claimed the tiny colt as his.

The king deliberated on this matter for a long time. "Did you actually see your mare give birth to the colt?" he asked. The peddler had to admit that he had not. "So you cannot swear that this foal is your mare's. Since the farmer found the colt beneath his wagon, I rule that it is his to keep."

Outside the palace, the farmer left with the colt tied to the back of his wagon. The peddler's mare neighed pitifully and struggled to follow her baby. The peddler tried his best to quiet her, but she was inconsolable. The mare's cries were heard by the queen in her garden, and she sent one of her ladies-in-waiting to find the cause of the disturbance. When the queen summoned the peddler to her and heard his tale, her dark eyes flashed but she did not smile.

Manka thought on the matter for a moment. Then she whispered something to the peddler. He bobbed his head and grinned as he listened, then bowed low and hurried off.

The next morning, as the king was taking his daily ride in the royal park, he saw the peddler sitting by the stable gate, holding a fishing line over a bucket. When the king asked him what he was doing, the peddler said that he was fishing for trout.

"Fishing for trout in a bucket? What sort of fool are you, man?"

The peddler replied, "Your Majesty, if a wagon can give birth to a foal, then I ought to be able to catch trout in this bucket."

The king narrowed his eyes. He knew immediately that the peddler had not come up with this answer on his own. At last the man confessed that the queen had told him what to say.

Now, even the cleverest of us make mistakes. But it takes a wise man to admit that he was wrong and make amends. The king saw to it that the colt was returned to its mother, and the peddler was given a handful of silver for his trouble.

Still, in matters of the heart, pride can blind even the wise. The king summoned his wife to their private chambers. Manka admitted that, yes, she had counseled the peddler and therefore, yes, she had broken their marriage agreement. Though it broke his heart to do it, the king decreed that Manka must leave the palace, return to her home, and be queen no more.

Neither of them spoke, but tears spattered the floor at their feet. At last, Manka raised her head and looked him in the eye.

"My king," Manka said softly, "before I go, grant me two small requests. Let me enjoy one last meal with you, and promise me that I may take from our marriage the one thing I hold most dear."

The king agreed, and Manka ordered a feast the likes of which no one in that palace had ever seen—leeks drenched in walnut syrup and dilled cabbage soup awash with dumplings, pork stuffed with currants and apples and saffron, baked hare and roast swan, rye bread, almond cream, damson tarts, and spicy gingered pears. And with every course, Manka and the king toasted one another and drained their goblets. Rather, the king did. Manka discreetly emptied her wine into a pouch at her side.

After several hours, the king reeled forward and collapsed on the table. Manka kissed his cheek, stroked his curls, and went to pack her bags.

When the king awoke, he was lying in a small room on a straw-filled pallet, covered with woolen blankets. Manka sat on a wooden stool at his side.

He sat up and demanded to know where he was.

"You are in Sebanov, in my home, darling."

When the king protested at being taken from the palace, Manka reminded him of his promise.

The young man sputtered. "What promise? To let you get me dead drunk and then kidnap me?"

"No, my darling. You promised me that I could take what I held most dear from our marriage. Did you ever doubt what that would be?"

Manka's husband looked at her for a long time. Then he burst out laughing.

"Manka, you are the cleverest person I have ever known. And I am the biggest fool. From this day forth, you shall sit at my side in my council chamber, and we will rule together."

So they returned to the palace and ruled together, and the kingdom prospered under their care. Till the end of their days, Manka and the king enjoyed their love for one another, which is truly the sweetest thing in the world.

Isn't it odd that every quality we value in our partners also has the tendency to disturb or annoy us? A witty husband can be great fun at parties, but your pride can suffer when he teases you. A calm, assertive wife is a welcome aid in an emergency, but her ability can feel threatening when she tries to advise you. In relationships, our capacity to accept our partners is largely determined by how readily we accept ourselves—our weaknesses as well as our strengths.

Easy recognition of our limitations rarely happens in real life—or fairy tales for that matter!—but it is knowledge worth having. In the realm of the fairy tale and folktale, the heroine or hero must learn through trial and error, for it would severely diminish the value and attraction of the story if every Jack and Ashenputtel knew their flaws at the outset and then heeded the advice given to them without question.

In our lives, we usually end up learning by trial and error, too. We are often either blind to our shortcomings or refuse to admit to them. That's a heavy burden to carry into a relationship. And an unnecessary one as well, for when we are humble enough to acknowledge our weak spots, our partners can come to our aid with their strength and love. It's such a relief, knowing you don't have to be mistress or master of every situation.

Who Knows What Could Happen?

IRAQ

Zahida was married to a merchant who sold carpets. Every day, Hasan went to his shop and smiled amiably at the people who came to purchase his wares. He even had a smile for the ones who did not buy, for you never know when a browser might come back and become a customer.

But when Hasan went home at night, often he did not smile. He frowned. He scowled and sneered. He grumbled and ground his teeth. And when Zahida spoke to him, he snapped at her, no matter what she said. He had a very difficult temperament.

Zahida didn't understand her husband's ill nature. Surely *she* meant more to him than the people who bought his carpets? After all, if he could be pleasant to strangers, why couldn't he be kind to his own wife?

One evening he came home more upset than usual. Hasan slammed the door, kicked over a stool, and yelled at Zahida for losing his slippers. Zahida considered making a few remarks about his eyesight, his memory, and his appalling lack of manners. But she knew her husband well.

"O my husband, sometimes you are in a bit of a temper when you come home at night. What angers you so?"

"The customers paw through my carpets and unroll them all over the shop. They drop crumbs in the woolen carpets and smear their greasy hands on the silken ones. And then they want me to sell them a rug for the price of a fig! Some days it's nothing but trouble. Why shouldn't I be in a bad mood?"

Zahida considered pointing out that *she* did not drop crumbs, haggle over prices, or cause him any trouble at all. But she knew her husband well. Instead, she nodded sympathetically and agreed that he had good cause to be irritated. Then she asked if he could give her a sign when he turned down their lane in the evenings, so she would know when he was vexed.

Hasan thought this was a reasonable request. He said that he would turn the tassel on his fez whenever he came home annoyed. That would be his signal for Zahida, and when she saw that tassel hanging down in front of his face she would know that he might say or do things that were rude and thoughtless, but he didn't really mean them and she shouldn't take them to heart.

As a compliant, dutiful wife, Zahida readily agreed to this arrangement. Then she said, "But what shall we do when *I* am in a foul mood? Because you know, my husband, I am easily rankled too. Some days the lentils burn, the cat falls into the well, and your mother gives me the recipe for your favorite lamb dish three times in one visit. It's nothing but aggravation from sunrise to sundown."

Hasan suggested that she put on her white apron and stand outside the door on such an evening. That would be her signal for him, and he would know that she might say or do things that were rash and ill advised, but she didn't really mean them and he shouldn't take them to heart.

At dusk the next day, Hasan charged through the city streets. Zahida stood behind the curtain at their front window, waiting for his approach. The moment she saw him turn down their lane, she tied her white apron strings behind her back, stepped outside and crossed her arms over her bosom. The tassel on Hasan's fez looked like a mare's tail when she's plagued by flies. With every step he took the strands bobbed before his eyes, and this only made him angrier.

But when Hasan saw Zahida, he stopped in his tracks. The tassel whacked him on the nose. Zahida frowned. Her husband's lip quivered. Neither one said a word. Hasan rocked back on his heels and swung the tassel over to the edge of his fez. Then he took a deep breath and smiled wanly. His wife moved aside and he entered the house without a word.

Later that week, Hasan had another trying day. He came boring down on that little house of theirs like a sandstorm. Zahida was ready for him; she flung on her white apron and stood before the door, glowering. Hasan slowed down and gulped—

and slapped the tassel away from his nose. The two eyed each other in silence for a moment, then he smiled weakly and they went into the house.

Yet a third time Hasan came home in a foul humor. And there was his wife glaring from the doorway, the white apron blinding him. Hasan mumbled something under his breath and flicked the tassel over to the side of his fez.

After a wordless meal, Hasan cleared his throat. "Zahida, my wife, this is most strange. For whenever I come home in a temper, you, too, have had a trying day. Of course I must put aside my own distress then, for it would never do for both of us to be upset at the same time. Who knows what could happen—I might strike you, you might throw a pot at my head."

Zahida nodded her head slowly, put down her coffee cup carefully, and looked at Hasan solemnly. "This *is* a terrible dilemma, my husband . . . If you must put aside your anger every time *I* am upset, and I must be calm and pleasant whenever *you* are in a bad mood, who knows what could happen—perhaps neither of us will ever be angry again."

Hasan looked at Zahida. She gazed back at him steadily. Then he narrowed his eyes, for he knew his wife well.

"O my wife, you are right. We must be very careful from now on. When a husband can brush aside his anger with a flick of his hand and a wife can be as cunning as a fox—who knows what else could happen."

Slowly, they both began to smile.

"She knew her husband well."

Such a simple little statement, such a profound achievement. It takes a long, long time to know someone well. A patient pair of ears, a keen pair of eyes, and a truly dedicated heart are required to understand your beloved. It takes even longer to align your responses with what you know about your partner's temperament. You can spy a pothole coming a mile away when you're in the heat of an argument and yet still march right into it, directly and defiantly. And you will stumble and fall and skin your knee every time without fail.

Some folks cannot be confronted directly about a problem. I know, I know, this violates all the rules of accountability and responsibility that are supposed to govern successful communication. But this is a world full of flawed, fragile people, and sometimes it's easier to let your partner discover the damaging effects of the problem at their own pace. Keeping quiet when you're itching to speak is quite a feat. Believe me, I know from firsthand experience! I have an impulsive tongue—"foot-in-mouth disease," I call it. It's caused me a lot of frustration, especially during arguments.

One of the greatest gifts I have cultivated over the years is the choice to witness. As my discernment has evolved, I've been able to sense the moments when my perspective shifts from "Meliss, who's got to be right" to "Meliss, who is an understanding partner." It actually feels as if my consciousness takes a step back from the fray. In those moments, I've learned that it is wiser to hold my tongue and wait till my temper (or his) cools off before discussing a problem—or not, as the case may warrant.

Pay attention. Please remember to take care of yourself and give your partner (and yourself) some room to breathe. Though your present tribulations might feel as if they demand immediate resolution, in truth you have many years together to work out a mutually agreeable, stable union.

Strawberries

CHEROKEE, NORTH AMERICA

Long ago, in the very first days of the world, there lived the first man and the first woman. They lived together as husband and wife, and they loved one another dearly.

But one day, they quarreled. Although neither later could remember what the quarrel was about, the pain grew stronger with every word that was spoken, until finally, in anger and in grief, the woman left their home and began walking away—to the east, toward the rising sun.

The man sat alone in his house. But as time went by, he grew lonelier and lonelier. The anger left him and all that remained was a terrible grief and despair, and he began to cry.

A spirit heard the man crying and took pity on him. The spirit said, "Man, why do you cry?"

The man said, "My wife has left me."

The spirit said, "Why did your woman leave?"

The man just hung his head and said nothing.

The spirit asked, "You quarreled with her?"

And the man nodded.

"Would you quarrel with her again?" asked the spirit.

The man said, "No." He wanted only to live with his wife as they had lived before—in peace, in happiness, and in love.

"I have seen your woman," the spirit said. "She is walking to the east toward the rising sun."

The man followed his wife, but he could not overtake her. Everyone knows an angry woman walks fast.

Finally, the spirit said, "I'll go ahead and see if I can make her slow her steps."

So the spirit found the woman walking, her footsteps fast and angry and her gaze fixed straight ahead. There was pain in her heart.

The spirit saw some huckleberry bushes growing along the trail, so with a wave of his hand, he made the bushes burst into bloom and ripen into fruit. But the woman's gaze remained fixed. She looked neither to the right nor the left, and she didn't see the berries. Her footsteps didn't slow.

Again, the spirit waved his hand, and one by one, *all* of the berries growing along the trail burst into bloom and ripened into fruit. But still, the woman's gaze remained fixed. She saw nothing but her anger and pain, and her footsteps didn't slow.

And again, the spirit waved his hand, and, one by one, the trees of the forest—the peach, the pear, the apple, the wild cherry—burst into bloom and ripened into fruit. But still, the woman's eyes remained fixed, and even still, she saw nothing but her anger and pain. And her footsteps didn't slow.

Then finally, the spirit thought, "I will create an entirely new fruit—one that grows very, very close to the ground so the woman must forget her anger and bend her head for a moment." So the spirit waved his hand, and a thick green carpet began to grow along the trail. Then the carpet became starred with tiny white flowers, and each flower gradually ripened into a berry that was the color and shape of the human heart.

As the woman walked, she crushed the tiny berries, and the delicious aroma came up through her nose. She stopped and looked down, and she saw the berries. She picked one and ate it, and she discovered its taste was as sweet as love itself. So she began walking slowly, picking berries as she went, and as she leaned down to pick a berry, she saw her husband coming behind her.

The anger had gone from her heart, and all that remained was the love she had always known. So she stopped for him, and together, they picked and ate the berries. Finally, they returned to their home where they lived out their days in peace, happiness, and love.

And that's how the world's very first strawberries brought peace between men and women in the world, and why to this day they are called the berries of love.

For me, this is a story about forgiveness. I love associating the sweetness of strawberries with the sweetness of forgiveness. Then again, there are times when I could use something with a much longer season to serve me as a reminder of its importance. I'd like a symbol that captures my attention every day of the year. I need to associate forgiveness with a slice of bread or a grain of rice.

Forgiving someone takes a big heart. When Tom hurts me, I become angry and upset and the last thing I want to do is forgive him. Still, I can only hold onto my resentment for so long. I don't pretend to be fine when I'm not; but I do try to clear the air as soon as possible. Ruth Bell Graham says, "A good marriage is the union of two good forgivers." How very true!

We cannot be forgiven until we have the humility and courage to say "I'm sorry." Apologizing is one of the scariest things you can do in a relationship. You make yourself very vulnerable and you never know beforehand if your apology will be accepted. You risk being stung by a cruel rebuff. Worst of all, you are admitting that you were at fault, you were wrong, you did something hurtful—and you know it.

What I've discovered over the years is that forgiveness becomes much easier the longer you're in a relationship. And when you can trust your partner to accept your apology graciously, saying "I'm sorry" becomes easier to do. It's never easy on your pride, but it is a balm to your integrity and to your heart.

Keep Your Wife Well Fed

SWAHILI, KENYA

Long ago in the Land of the Zanj, the sultan's wife, Jamila, fell ill. Day after day she lay abed, her lovely face turned to the wall, her body wasted and weak. The palace cooks prepared their most tempting dishes for their mistress. Though she dutifully ate them, she only sighed and grew thinner. The wisest healers were consulted, but none of their remedies worked. The most powerful priests were summoned to drive away evil demons from her heart, yet still Jamila languished. The sultan was gravely perturbed, for it was unthinkable that the wife of the most powerful ruler in the land should be ill and that he could not make her well.

At last the sultan sent a proclamation to every town, hamlet, and port of call along the Swahili Coast: anyone who could heal his wife would be given his weight in nuggets of raw gold. If they failed, however, they would be put to death.

Despite such a consequence, the lure of gold overpowered the wits of even the most sensible of men. They came to Mombasa from near and far to try their luck and win the reward. Jamila was given roasted lion heart to eat and cow's milk and blood to drink. Men chanted, danced, and leapt around her bed; they tied smelly goatskin pouches around her middle. She was poked and rubbed at midday, greased and scrubbed by the light of the moon, shaken and told to say *"Kitoweo na mchuzi, kitoweo na mchuzi* (meat and gravy, meat and gravy)" while facing the rising sun. Nothing worked. The poor woman remained prostrate, whittled away to skin and bones. The sultan had the fools beheaded and then went to sit beside his wife's bed. He had lost all patience with her mysterious malady.

"What is the matter with you, woman? I have given you everything you could possibly need! You have combs of ivory and slippers of gazelle leather. You bathe in rose water and eat from plates of beaten silver. Each of your serving women is the daughter of a chief . . . and *I* am your husband!"

Jamila was too weak to answer by this time, but she tried to smile. A thin tear slid down her hollow cheek, and she sniffed.

Just then, there was a commotion at the door of Jamila's bedchamber. The royal vizier slipped in and whispered to the sultan, and he nodded impatiently. A poor wood-worker named Hamisi was ushered into the room and bowed low before his ruler.

"Your Greatness, I have two words I want to say to you. I have heard that your wife is very ill. Would you permit me to see her for one hour? I may be able to help her."

The sultan waved his hand dismissively at Jamila.

"If you are fool enough to think that you can do anything for this woman, you may try." He stalked from the room, and Hamisi was left alone with the sultan's wife.

In a matter of ten minutes, the woodworker stood before the sultan again. "Your Eminence, I have two words I want to say to you. I believe I have found the cause of all your wife's troubles. The cure is very simple. You must feed her meat of the tongue. If you will do this every day for three weeks, she should soon be hearty and well again."

The sultan thanked Hamisi and vowed that he would do as he suggested. The vizier asked the fellow where he lived in order to reward him when Jamila recovered— or to punish him if she worsened. At once the sultan commanded his royal hunters to kill a rhinoceros, an elephant, and a giraffe, since they each had large tongues. In the palace kitchen, the royal cooks were ordered to prepare the tongues in every pos-sible way—boiled in fish broth and roasted with pumpkin, stuffed with rice and baked over millet, simmered with beans and stewed in mango juice. Then the royal vizier was ordered to serve these dishes to the ailing woman every day and report on her progress.

Imagine how disappointed the sultan was when he heard that Jamila had eaten each and every dish, yet after three weeks she still remained as thin and pallid as ever. The woodworker was summoned before the sultan.

"Your cure was as worthless as all the others, you scoundrel. You shall be beheaded."

"Wait, wait, Your Wiseness," Hamisi said. "I have two words I want to say to you. Are you certain you followed my directions exactly?"

"Yes, of course!"

Hamisi frowned, clearly puzzled. "And you yourself gave it to her?"

The sultan stammered. "Why, er, no, actually it was my vizier who took it to her but—"

"Well, that is the problem, Your Graciousness. It is most important that you yourself give her the meat of the tongue."

The sultan grumbled, but he released Hamisi. The next day he, the sultan himself, carried a covered golden tray to his wife's room and cut up fried elephant tongue in tiny slivers and fed it to her. But things got no better. Jamila ate every morsel then moaned and turned her face to the wall. The sultan was outraged.

The woodworker was dragged before him in chains this time.

"Your scheme has failed, Hamisi. Jamila is still scrawny as a cat. You will die today!"

"Wait, wait, Your Keenness," cried Hamisi. "I have two words I want to say to you. Perhaps I can cure her myself. It is most unusual, but who knows, perhaps if I take her to my home, she will recover more quickly. However, my own wife will complain, so we must trade wives."

The sultan was secretly relieved to have Jamila taken away from him so that he would no longer have to see her gaunt body and mournful eyes. A royal litter was ordered, and she was carried off to the outskirts of the city where Hamisi lived with his wife. Jamila was left on a reed mat in the corner of the small, mud-coated hut. Hamisi's wife, Henzerani, was bundled into the litter with tasseled cushions and a silk-covered canopy and taken back to the palace.

In three weeks' time, the woodworker's wife was thinner and more haggard than Jamila had ever been! The sultan was beside himself. He was determined to seize the wily Hamisi and have him punished.

Under cover of night, he and his vizier traveled to Hamisi's thatched hut. They peeked in through the window and there they saw a beautiful woman, sleek and plump as a young girl, glowing with health and happiness. She was rubbing palm oil on her skin and humming to herself. Then they looked more carefully, and they realized that this smiling lady was the sultan's wife, Jamila!

And there was Hamisi, sitting on the mat across from her and speaking in a high, singsong voice: "—and so the little monkey said to the shark, 'Oh, what a shame you didn't tell me sooner that your wife wanted to eat my heart. Then I would have brought it with me. But alas, dear friend, my heart remains behind in the tree where you saw me today. Don't you know, monkeys always leave their hearts in the tops of palm trees?'"

Jamila chuckled and leaned forward. "Then what happened, my husband? That fool of a shark didn't take him back to the shore, did he?"

"Oh yes, oh yes, he did, dear wife." And as Hamisi finished the story, Jamila slapped her knees and grinned. "Some people never learn, eh?"

Then Hamisi told her of a mighty ship he had seen in the harbor that week, come all the way from China, tall as the spire on the sultan's highest tower and twice as long as the palace walls. He had watched the merchants unpack their goods: cups as clear as well water and beads that shone like wet seashells, bowls the color of pale spring grass and a strange round disk with markings all around the edge. There was an arrow on the disk that always pointed toward Malindi, no matter which way the merchant turned it.

"What was it for, Hamisi? What did it do?"

"It was a great magic, Jamila. The sailors said the captain used one to keep their ship on course."

Jamila shook her head in wonder.

Next he told her about his friend, Asim the fisherman, who caught a fish and brought it home for dinner, and when he cut it open there was a golden ring inside the fish's belly.

"And so what did he do with the ring, my husband?"

"Well, first he thought he might take it to the sultan of Benadir, to see if he could claim a reward. But then he thought no, the sultan might just take it and give him nothing. Then he thought he would take it to the market and trade it for a new boat with the sails painted yellow. But then he thought no, he might not find a boat as sturdy as the old one he already had. So then he gave it to his wife and told her it was a magic ring. He said that she could make a wish and the ring would bring her anything she asked for. But only one wish, he told her. Only one wish."

Jamila's eyes grew wide and she begged him to tell her what Asim's wife wished for.

"Oh, old Miriam hasn't wished for anything yet, and she probably never will. She'll think of something, but then she'll change her mind, because, you know, Jamila, she only wants to ask for the *perfect* thing."

Then he sang a silly song about the hippo and why he twirls his tail, and Jamila held her sides and tears rolled down her cheeks. She squealed for him to stop, stop, but the sultan and the vizier could tell she didn't truly want him to stop. Hamisi and Jamila lay on the mat, waving their feet in the air and laughing.

At that moment, the sultan stormed into the bare little hut. He commanded Jamila to return to the palace, but she refused to go. She said that she intended to stay with Hamisi, where she was content and well fed.

"Well fed? What do you mean, woman? I don't see a grain of millet in the house."

Hamisi spoke cheerfully. "Oh, we have food enough to keep us alive, Your Astuteness. I think that Jamila means the meat of my tongue, that which I share with her every day. There are few things better to keep a woman happy."

The sultan had no choice but to give Hamisi his weight in gold—and to marry Henzerani. In time, she became *almost* as plump and sleek and glowing as Jamila, the woodworker's happy wife.

The dilemma of this story can be a problem for even the most communicative couples. In the first flush of romance, we want to share everything with our lovers. Everything. We are deliriously obsessed with one another. Gradually though, the central focus of our lives shifts from solely "the couple" to include anything and everything else. To a degree this shift is inevitable, for we all earn a living, have friends and family, and enjoy other interests. Many of us have children, and raising them can become an all-consuming task. However, to keep our unions healthy and happy, our lover's satisfaction must always remain a vital priority.

I used to have this notion that if Tom and I worked long and hard enough on our relationship, eventually it would reach a point of maturity and satisfaction where it gelled. We could then check RELATIONSHIP *off of our list of things to do and coast home, living off the fruits of our previous labors. Alas, that is not how it works. We discovered that a relationship requires diligent attention. If I become too distracted—by our daughter, my career, family obligations, what have you— then Tom notices. He misses me even when I am close by, because our connection has come unraveled.*

The tricky part of this problem is that it is often so insidious. The connection unravels slowly—one less kiss, one less "thank you," one less funny story shared at bedtime—and often even the partner being shortchanged hardly notices the gradual withdrawal of time and attention until it is far gone. Some couples avoid this subtle erosion by consciously sharing time every day, or at least on a regular basis, to be certain that the threads stay wound securely. Of course there are times when compromises must be made, and there will be temporary shortfalls of connectedness, but this tale reminds us that we always deserve our partner's best—and that our partner deserves our best as well.

Saint Peter's Blessings

CUBA

One day Saint Peter was out walking with his good friend, Saint Theresa. It was a hot summer day, and even saints can become thirsty, so Saint Peter knocked on the door of a house nearby. A smiling woman answered. When the strangers on her doorstep asked for some water, she graciously invited them into her tidy little home, seated them in her most comfortable chairs, and offered them tall glasses brimming with clear, cool water.

As the two visitors prepared to leave, Saint Peter held up his hand in blessing. "May you have a bad husband." The poor woman was so startled by the man's comment that she said nothing as they left.

Saint Theresa was puzzled. "Saint Peter, why in Heaven's name did you wish a bad husband on that sweet, kind woman? Surely she deserves a prince!"

Peter merely shook his head and did not reply.

The saints continued their walk as cicadas shrilled from the trees. Heat rippled across the roadway, and again they felt their mouths grow dry. Saint Peter approached another house and rapped on the door and a woman answered. When he asked for water, she curtsied and cheerfully beckoned them in and then filled two sparkling clean glasses from a china pitcher. The weary travelers sat in her immaculate kitchen as they cooled their throats. The fragrance of basil swept through the room from her dooryard garden, the hearth tiles gleamed, and canaries trilled from a perch in a shady corner.

As the two visitors prepared to leave this woman, Saint Peter again held up his hand in blessing. "May you have a bad husband." The woman gasped at the stranger's words, then quickly crossed herself.

Saint Theresa was bewildered. "Saint Peter, has the heat stewed your mind? Do you know what you just said? You wished that lovely lady a bad husband! What kind of a blessing is that?"

Peter still did not reply.

The day wore on. The road burned through the soles of their sandals, and sweat streaked their faces. Saint Peter and Saint Theresa came to a house with a broken-down fence around a yard full of weeds. When Saint Peter knocked on the door of the hut, a woman's harsh voice came from within, "*Momentito, momentito!* I'm busy!"

They heard her muttering all the way to the door, complaining about inconsiderate strangers who bothered her every hour of the day and night. The door opened on rusty hinges, just enough for the woman to poke her head out to see who had come.

"What do you want?"

You would have thought those two had demanded hot meals and feather beds from the sour look she gave them, but saints can be exceedingly charming, so at last she consented to get them water. The woman left them standing outside in the heat while she went off to her kitchen, slamming doors and scolding a cat who'd gotten underfoot. After a long wait, she returned with two cracked mugs half full of tepid water. Saint Peter and Saint Theresa thanked her heartily for her generosity.

Before Saint Peter turned to leave the tumbledown house, he raised his hand in blessing. "May you have a good husband." The woman laughed in his face.

Saint Theresa was astonished. "Saint Peter, Saint Peter, surely you have gone mad. That woman is a wretch! And you gave *her* the good husband?! I'm going to speak to the Lord about you. You're a menace to marriage!"

Saint Peter turned to Saint Theresa and smiled mysteriously but said nothing.

Before Theresa could go to Heaven to make her complaint to the Lord, she was distracted by a request for help from a poor mortal in her care, and the saints parted company. But one summer's day a year later they were out walking again, and Saint Theresa pointed to a house on the side of the road. "Isn't that the place where we stopped for water last summer, Peter? I wonder if that sweet lady ever married."

Saint Peter knocked on the door as Saint Theresa held her breath, and a smiling man answered the door. They were welcomed into the same tidy little kitchen and again given the best chairs and tall glasses of water. After awhile the woman came in. She had been in the village, selling her weaving. As they chatted, Saint Peter asked, "And are you happy with your husband, my daughter?"

The woman nodded. "Oh *si, si!* He is a wonderful man." Then she shook her head. "But at first I did not think so. You see, we both work all day long, but he expected me to do all the housework and cooking, too. No matter how often I asked him to help, he just lay in his hammock every evening and watched me make his meals and wash his shirts. I wondered why the Lord had sent me such a lazy good-for-nothing.

"But I didn't give up on him! No . . . I just stopped doing the cooking and washing and cleaning. I strung myself a hammock next to his, and every evening we swung back and forth, back and forth. We ate raw beans and drank water, and he wore the same shirt every day for a week, two weeks, three weeks. And every night we swung back and forth, back and forth. He would glare at me and I would smile at him. But oh, good sir, every night I would pray to our sweet Mother Mary for help.

"And then one day when I came home, I smelled rice cooking. The kitchen floor was swept, and the bed was made. We had our supper, then we washed up the dishes. And *then* we got up in our hammocks and we swung back and forth, back and forth, together."

The two saints continued on their way and soon arrived at the home of the next woman they had visited. They could hear a baby crying within as Saint Peter knocked at the door. A handsome man welcomed them into the same cheery kitchen where the tiles gleamed, the canaries sang, and the woman sat nursing a young baby. After the saints had been served their water, they fell to chatting with the young couple, and Saint Peter asked the wife, "Does your husband make you happy, my child?"

She smiled and glanced fondly at the man beside her. "I love him with all my heart now, good sir, but it was not always like that." She told them how her husband used to look at the other ladies, always had a smile or a wink for the pretty ladies in town. "No matter what I said or did, he just wouldn't stop. I used to think I'd like to give our dear Lord a piece of my mind, sending me a rascal like that.

"Well, one evening in the middle of the week he came home and I had a big chicken dinner, a real feast, all ready for him. When he asked me what the party was for, I told him, 'No party, this is a wake for our rooster.' I said I found that rooster over in the neighbor's henhouse almost every day, and I told him, 'I don't want a rooster who won't keep his own hens happy. There's more than enough to keep him busy right here in his own back yard, don't you think?' And then I took my two sharpest carving knives and sliced him off a real big chunk of that bird and put it on his plate."

The husband cuddled their baby under his chin and grinned sheepishly. "She was right. *More* than enough."

It was nearing sundown as they came to the home of the third woman. The fence was repaired and whitewashed, lilies bloomed in the front garden, and there was fresh paint on the shutters. Saint Peter knocked on the door and it was immediately opened by the same woman, now smiling broadly. She flung the door open wide and ushered them in to her kitchen where she carefully polished her two best glasses and filled them with fresh, cold water.

As Peter and Theresa sat, a man came in the back door and greeted them. The wife offered her guests fruit, and while they ate, Saint Peter chatted with her.

"And are you happy with your husband, my child?" he asked mildly.

The couple exchanged glances and laughed. The woman said *"Si, si, muy alegre,"* then admitted that it was not always so. She told him that when they first married, she used to yell at him and call him names and criticize everything he did. But that smart husband of hers, oooh, he made her so mad, because he never yelled back, he never called her names. No, whenever she started being mean to him, he just went out to the barn and saddled his horse and rode off. Then he would come back in a little while and ask if she would like to *talk* to him. She said sometimes he rode off four or five times a day, till she finally decided she would try *talking* to him instead of yelling at him.

Later, as Saint Peter and Saint Theresa walked down the moonlit road, Theresa grinned at her friend. "I beg your pardon, Peter. You are indeed a wise fellow. I will never doubt your blessings again."

Saint Peter chuckled. "It is a miracle, isn't it, Theresa? How these mortals find one another, just the right one for her, just the right one for him. And when they do, how hard they resist my blessing. He tries to make her do this, she tries to make him say that. But in the end, when they understand, aaah, then it is so sweet. Like a little piece of Heaven come down to Earth.

"And that makes my work easier, Theresa. For when one couple understands each another, others see that. They want to be like them. They try harder in their own marriages. It is a miracle."

Saint Peter and Saint Theresa flew off into the night sky, up toward Heaven. Saint Theresa looked back over her shoulder, down at the countryside they had walked through that day. Far below, she picked out the little house they had just left.

"*Si*, Peter," she said softly. "It is a miracle."

Why, you ask. Why, you whine. Why, you shout. Why did I pick this person who provokes me and disappoints me and criticizes me? Wasn't she supposed to be my dream come true? Wasn't he supposed to be my soulmate?

I like this story's answer as well as any. She is your blessing. He will teach you the lessons you need to learn about respect and forgiveness and humility and—well, you probably know what you are learning better than I do, eh?

It took a very long time for me to believe this, but it is true: you cannot change someone else, you can only change yourself. (Sometimes changing yourself may mean acting on your own behalf and leaving a hurtful partnership. It's a drastic but sometimes necessary step.) When I notice myself becoming upset with Tom's behavior, I know that I have a choice about how to respond to it. I can't "save" him or "fix" him, even though I'd love to try. Instead, I've got to change something that I'm doing. Remarkably, that usually shifts things quickly and before too long we're back in balance again.

Over the years, as I have struggled to understand and learn from my soulmate, the phrase "hold fast" has helped me to stay the course. It comes from a breathtakingly romantic Scottish folktale, "Tamlin," about a young woman who rescues her beloved from the clutches of the fairy folk. The fairies transform Tamlin into a series of frightening, vile creatures and dangerous things in their effort to break Janet's embrace of her lover. But Tamlin has warned her of their trickery and bids her to "hold fast, hold fast no matter what happens to me." She does, and eventually she wins him back, in his human form, forever free of the fairies' spell.

I have a much healthier, more satisfying relationship because of all the times I have gritted my teeth and held fast, trusting that underneath that bear's growl or snake's hiss is the true love I cherish. It's not romantic—it's very hard work. But it's worth it. Blessings always are.

What Women Most Desire

ENGLAND

In the days when Arthur was high king and Guinevere was his queen, the finest knight in all the land was Sir Gawain. He was heir to the throne, son of Arthur's sister, beloved by the knights of the Round Table and the ladies of the court. Those were times of sorcery and secrets, treachery and illusion, and Arthur was glad for a companion as trustworthy as his own nephew.

In the autumn of the year, the king and all his court would go hunting in the untamed, trackless northlands. Arthur and his men chased boars and stags through forests of towering oak and ash and beech. Gawain always rode at his uncle's side, but one day the king pursued a magnificent buck into a thicket and disappeared. Gawain and his brothers and the other knights tried to follow, but Inglewood Forest was unyielding—there was no path into the trees. They shouted Arthur's name to no avail; he did not respond to their calls.

The king was drawn deeper into the close-set trees and tangled vines until he was unable to ride any further, so he dismounted and pressed on. Across a small clearing, the deer's white tail winked out of sight as it leapt over a fallen tree. Before Arthur could follow, a man burst into the glade and blocked his way. Now Arthur was a big man, but he was dwarfed by the stranger before him. The man was covered in coarse leather leggings and shirt and a rough woven cloak of dull green. His bare feet were stained the color of the earth, leaves matted his dark hair and beard, and his black eyes glinted as he stared at the king. Over his head he held a knotted, burled club, full half his height, streaked with rusty red.

The man snarled one word—"Arthur"—and swung at him. Arthur fell, but he was a warrior as well as a king. He rolled onto his back, jumped to his feet, and crouched, ready to defend himself barehanded. The stranger sneered as he raised the club high.

"Who are you?" Arthur gasped.

"I am called Sir Gromer, King, and lately these lands you ride were mine. Now, I am told, they are yours." The menace in the knight's voice twisted Arthur's stomach.

"And what do you want?" Arthur asked, eyeing the gnarled wooden staff above him.

"Ah there, *now* ye ask it of me," he said quietly. "Now . . . when my lands are no longer mine and I have no home." He snarled once again. "I want your life, King. I want you *dead.* But I'll not have it said that I killed an unarmed man."

He lowered the club—and Arthur exhaled. "I'll pose you a riddle instead, and your life rides on the answer. Agreed?"

He had no choice; Arthur agreed.

"Swear an oath to me, Arthur. Swear that you will return here, to this place, in a year and a day, with the answer to my question."

"I do swear."

Sir Gromer leaned over, leering at Arthur, and hissed, "Then tell me this, King, *What is it that women most desire?*"

Arthur repeated the question. "I will return, Sir Gromer, with the answer to your riddle. You have my word."

The king lost no time in recovering his horse and rejoining his men. Only Gawain noticed Arthur's knuckles, white on the reins, and his cheeks, drained of color. Back at Carlisle Castle, Gawain followed his uncle to his chambers and questioned him. Arthur told him of the strange meeting with Sir Gromer. "I swore, Gawain, that I would have the answer, and I will. I shall find what it is that women most desire."

The two men mused on how to learn the true answer to the riddle, and then Gawain devised a plan. They would each travel half the kingdom and ask every woman they met what she most desired. They would record the answers and then meet back at the castle in a year, where Arthur would choose the reply that he deemed best.

And so it was. Gawain set off the next morning, riding east. Arthur began by asking his noble lady Guinevere what she desired most.

Her answer was prompt.

"Why, to please you, my lord. In all ways."

Arthur laughed and kissed her, and he did not leave her chambers till midday, but he suspected that her answer was not the one Sir Gromer was seeking.

Next he asked the old abbess of the chapel in the castle. That good woman spoke with surety. "To serve the Lord our God with all our hearts and souls, Your Highness. That is what we women most desire."

Arthur thanked the abbess but left her certain that that was not an answer to satisfy the knight in the forest.

Gawain fared no better.

A serving woman at a tavern rubbed her back and sighed. "What I most desire is a bed, sir. A nice, soft, goose feather bed. Ah me, yes. And a tankard of ale and a joint of beef and a tray of sweet cakes to top it off. Ah, that would do for me. And what can I get for you now, Your Lordship?"

A pinch-faced widow scowled at him. "Land, my lad, and lots of it. Gold and jewels and silken dresses might do for some, but as for me, I'll take *land*."

And a saucy lady-in-waiting smirked at his question. "What do I most *desire*, Sir? Well, now, why don't you come to my chamber this evening and see?"

At the year's end, the two men met in the northern castle keep, where Arthur pored over rolls of parchment covered with women's dreams and wishes and longings. But as the cold afternoon light faded, he swept his arm across the table and the papers tumbled to the floor. Arthur paced the room and pointed at them.

"Not a word there will ransom my life."

Then he left the room, saddled his horse, and rode off alone toward Inglewood Forest. Arthur brooded, his eyes unseeing, his ears not hearing. His horse picked her way along a hillside path till she entered a stand of holly and oak. Sitting on a grey rock in the heart of the grove was a figure. Spying it, the mare twisted and reared and tried to bolt. It took all of Arthur's strength to get her in hand once more.

He looked down at the creature below. Arthur bit his lip to keep from crying out. She was a nightmare, this woman. It was not simply that she was ancient, her flesh grooved and sagging on her bones; that he could have borne. But her face and arms were burnt red and raw, her teeth were rotted stumps, and her hairless head oozed with pustules and bloody scabs. She squinted up at him with one eye, for the other socket was empty and caved in against her cheek. Still, she looked up at him steadily, without a blush, and spoke his name.

"Arthur."

The voice was low and harsh and rattled with phlegm. In all the forest there was no birdcall, no rustle of wind in the trees. Only that rasping, tortured sound.

"You are Arthur, and you have a question . . . And you do not know the answer to that question."

Every hair on Arthur's neck stood straight up.

"Who *are* you?"

She folded her clawlike hands in her lap. "I am called Lady Ragnell. And I hold the answer to your question."

Now, Arthur would not have long remained the king of all Britain had he not been a shrewd judge of men. And over the last year he had paid more attention to women than he ever had before. Looking into that bloodshot, lashless eye of hers, Arthur knew that this woman spoke the truth.

"My lady, if you will tell me the answer to this riddle, I will grant you anything your heart desires!"

She laughed. It was terrible to hear.

"Anything? Well, then, come you here, my lord King, and I will tell you the secret that will save your life."

The horse would not move a step closer and had to be tied to a tree. Arthur knelt beside the woman, and she caught his cloak. A raven cawed high overhead and broke the stillness as she bent her head towards his. The stench from her breath as she whispered in his ear almost choked him, but when she released his cloak, Arthur's mind was at ease for the first time in a year.

He bowed to Ragnell and took her hot, shriveled hand. "My good Lady Ragnell, I thank you with all my heart. And now I ask, what do you wish? What can I give you in return for this service? Would you like a chest of gold, a piece of land, a —?"

"I want your fairest knight, my lord. You must ask Sir Gawain if he would consent to marry me."

Arthur's stomach heaved. He turned very pale and then very red. "My dear Lady Ragnell, I cannot give Gawain to you. He is his own man."

Ragnell laughed again and Arthur shuddered.

"Only ask him, my King, that is all I wish. And if he consents, bring him to me tomorrow, as you go to meet Sir Gromer."

Arthur nodded once.

"You have my word, lady. I will ask him straightaway."

He left her there and galloped back to the castle.

Ah, but the telling of it to his nephew, the knight he loved like a son, the finest and noblest blood in all of Britain—he could not bring himself to do it! Gawain saw how troubled he was and supposed he still worried over the riddle's answer, so he let him be. But at last Arthur minded himself of his promise to Ragnell and called Gawain to his chambers.

He told the young man of his meeting with the woman in Inglewood and how she had provided him the answer that would ransom his life. Gawain cried with joy. Then Arthur told him that she had asked for something in return.

"As is only to be expected, Uncle. And what does she want, the poor soul, a purse of gold or a house or a bit of land?"

"You, Gawain. She wants only you. She bade me ask if you would consent to—to marry her." And here his voice broke and Arthur wept in sorrow and pity for them all.

Well, blood runs true. Gawain had pledged his life to Arthur as his liege lord. He stood silent for a moment, taking a deep breath, but when he spoke his voice was steady and firm.

"My lord Arthur, it would be an honor for me to marry the woman who has saved your life."

The next day, Arthur packed every one of the parchments in his saddle pouches in the hope that another answer would satisfy Gromer and release Gawain from his fate. They set off with a white palfrey for Ragnell, and Arthur left Gawain in the holly grove while he continued on into the forest.

The moment Arthur stepped into the clearing, Sir Gromer appeared from amid the trees, holding his monstrous club. Arthur calmly began reading from the first roll, but Gromer ripped the paper from his hands and growled, "You do not have the answer, Arthur, and now your life is mine. I am king and this land is mine once more!"

He lifted the club above his head, but Arthur stopped him with a raised hand.

"No! I *do* have the answer you seek."

And when he told Sir Gromer the words he had heard the day before, the knight roared and cursed in rage.

"You did not get that answer yourself! That hag Ragnell told you this! I will kill her when I find her!" And he flung the club across the clearing where it cracked a stout oak in two.

Arthur lost no time in leaving that place. He joined Gawain and found Lady Ragnell beside him. Together they made their way back to the castle.

Now, well you know that bad news travels faster than a hare pursued by a pack of hounds. So when Arthur and Gawain and Ragnell entered the castle courtyard, every woman, man, and child of the court and household was there to see them. The other knights stood slack-jawed in disbelief as they watched Ragnell ride by. Little children shrieked and buried their faces in their mothers' skirts, the unwed ladies of the court moaned in disappointment, and grown men turned their faces to the castle walls and gagged.

Sir Gawain rode calmly beside the lady and guided her to the chapel steps. Despite Arthur's protest that there was no need to hurry, Gawain insisted on the marriage immediately. There followed a wedding feast unlike any other.

No one had the heart for eating or dancing or merriment save Ragnell herself. She ate three capons, cracking their bones and sucking out the marrow before throwing the scraps to the hounds beneath her. She downed four tankards of ale, wiped her mouth on the cloth spread beneath the food, and belched so loudly that the dogs yipped in surprise. The new bride whispered lewd jokes to Guinevere, then stroked Gawain's thigh and squeezed his arm. "Will ye be strong enough to hold me tonight, husband?" she croaked. She pulled him to the middle of the hall, where they stumbled and lurched around as the musicians tried their best to play something sprightly. Throughout it all, Gawain was courteous and attentive to Lady Ragnell, while the other knights laid bets whether he would run himself through with his own sword before nightfall.

As night drew down, the newly wedded couple was led to their bridal chamber. Arthur and Guinevere gave them their blessing, the door was closed, and Gawain and Ragnell were left alone. Now, some say that they stood in darkness, while some say she blew out the candle, and still others say he just closed his eyes. But this I know: when Ragnell asked hoarsely, "Will you do your duty, husband? Will you kiss me?" and turned up her face to his, he did it.

For he was, in very truth, the finest knight that ever walked the land. And though he was yet young, Gawain had a shrewd knowing of men and animals—and of all that dwell in places wild and deep. He held his breath, to be sure, but he kissed his wife on her dry, cracked lips, and then he slipped his arms around her withered, reeking body and held her close for a moment.

When he released her, she laughed, but it was not the same sound that had curdled Arthur's blood. It was clear and rich as a lark's song in spring. She caught hold of his head and pressed her mouth to his again, and her breath was sweet as the scent of woodbine. Then she ran her hands up his chest and pressed her body against his, and at that moment Gawain was certain that this was not Lady Ragnell.

"Hold!" he cried, pushing her away. Gawain's hand flew to his side, but he wore no sword. He backed toward the door, straining to see anything he might use as a weapon.

"Who are you? What magic is this?"

Again she laughed, and then she spoke.

"I am your bride, your wife Ragnell. But before you kissed me, I was under a curse by my brother, whom your good King Arthur thwarted today with my aid."

And then she told him how Sir Gromer, her half brother, had cursed her for refusing his attentions, turning her into the hideous creature Gawain had first met in the holly grove. Gromer said that she would remain that way until the truest knight in Britain would willingly consent to marry her and make her his bride.

Gawain pulled the woman to the window and stared at her. By the light of a waxing moon, he saw that her face was no longer blighted. Her teeth were straight and her eyes gleamed. She had hair, dark and thick around her shoulders. Her mouth was moist on his cheek, his neck, his lips, and she murmured, "Truly, I am Ragnell."

The poor man nearly fainted with relief. Willingly he allowed himself to be kissed and held and caressed till his knees almost gave way with wanting her. Then he held her off at arm's length and asked, "But what happened to the other one?"

"There is no 'other one,' my husband. I tell you, I am Ragnell. With your kiss, his spell is half-broken, dear Gawain, but . . . but now you must choose. Will you have me fair by day, as I am this moment, amongst the lords and ladies of your court, and then foul again by night? Or would you have me come to you alone in our bedchamber, fair as you now see me, and then walk amongst your friends and companions as the foul one I was before? Choose carefully, Gawain."

Sir Gawain hesitated, staring at his new bride. But he was quiet only a moment before he laughed.

"My sweet lady, do you not know how many nights I laid out under the stars, wrapped in my saddle blankets, wondering desperately what women most desire? Now that I know, I cannot make this choice for you, it is for you alone to make.

"As you told Arthur, it is your sovereign right to choose, to do as you will in your life. And whether you will be fair by day or by night, I will abide by your decision and love you at all times."

"Oh Gawain!" she cried. "You have broken the spell completely! It is banished forever. Gromer said that if you guessed the secret of his riddle, he would have power over me no more. I am truly free. You will always behold me as I am now, your dearest, loving Ragnell."

And now we leave them to each other, for when two lovers unite, they need nothing more than each other to give them what *they* most desire.

The wondrous transformation in this tale never ceases to enchant me. The "kiss of sovereignty" is an archetypal ritual. Gawain is one of a legendary line of young Celtic heroes who chooses to embrace a mysterious woman who appears physically repulsive. When the man passes this test of faith, the hag is restored to her true self and the hero is revealed in his true nature—they both attain sovereignty. Literally, they become queen and king of the realm. We reenact this same ritual when we affirm our partner's autonomy, their right to choose.

Sir Gawain did the proper and honorable thing in marrying Lady Ragnell. He treated her courteously and behaved with dignity before his peers and his king. Yet her transformation did not occur until they were behind closed doors. In the privacy and intimacy of their room, he still chose to act with respect and tenderness toward a loathsome hag. Gawain was a man of integrity, and his goodness was rewarded when he accepted Ragnell as she was and then acknowledged her sovereignty.

Despite our best intentions and most careful preparations, we are still embarking on a risky journey when we vow to stay with another person till we are parted by death. Our lovers do not come with labels—SATISFACTION GUARANTEED OR YOUR MONEY BACK! Like Gawain and Ragnell, we must sometimes act on faith, with no sure knowledge of what is to come. There's no denying it; entering into a relationship is taking a leap into the unknown.

However, there are certain things you can depend upon. You will get out of your relationship what you put into it. When you consistently call forth and affirm someone's excellence, their true nature, they will rise to meet their own highest expectations. When you esteem someone as they are, the power of your unconditional love will transform them forever.

EPILOGUE

There is a tradition in southeastern England that has been honored for almost a thousand years. Originally, couples from the town of Little Dunmow and the surrounding area would come to the priory once a year to vie for a flitch of bacon. They had to convince a jury of six unmarried maidens and six unmarried men that they had not quarreled, disagreed, or said unkind things to one another in the previous year; in fact, they were not even permitted to have entertained the wish to be unmarried during that time.

When—or if—a blissful couple was selected, they swore a solemn oath (in verse) pledging their honesty while kneeling on a stone in the churchyard. Afterward, they received half of a hog, a flitch, as their reward, and they were hoisted up onto carved oak chairs and paraded through the village. Chaucer refers to the Dunmow flitch in *The Canterbury Tales.* The custom was more than two hundred years old then. The tradition continued unabated at the priory for centuries, and when the priory closed the townsfolk took up the ritual themselves. Though the ceremony has changed in modern times, to this day, you can go to Little Dunmow and present your case as a couple who has learned how to live happily ever after.*

Several hundred years ago, a gammon of bacon could help keep a family fed for months. It was a prize worth pursuing. Nowadays, it's much easier to buy a package of sliced bacon strips from the market than to work hard all year to keep your relationship in a state of perfection! In our culture, we no longer have to sustain a relationship in order to survive; we enter our relationships out of choice and maintain them out of love and devotion.

But wouldn't it be interesting to pretend that there *was* something greater at stake? Suppose that the health of your relationship was no less than a matter of life and death. Once a year you'd sit down together and take a look at how successful you'd been in

---

* http://www.saffire.org.uk/saffire/history/flitch.html

fulfilling your vows, whatever they happened to be. You'd evaluate your efforts as a couple and decide whether you had earned say, a pound of bacon—or the whole *hog!*

Are you and your beloved worthy of the Dunmow flitch?

I thought of winning that flitch often as I worked on this book. It was a tantalizing vision—to create a union that balanced and harmonious, to place the integrity of the relationship above the insistent little demands of the ego. When I told my friends and family about it, they all loved the legend but ruefully admitted that there was little chance of a flitch in their freezers, ever. I'm fairly certain Tom and I will never win the bacon either, but that won't stop me from trying. How could I settle for less?

As the book took shape, I was reminded of the old adage, "We teach what we most need to learn." On the one hand, I have been writing and telling stories on this subject for more than twenty years. I thought that surely I had mastered the lessons they offered long ago. Then again, I know how easily I get snagged on assumptions, so I tried to stay alert to what happened as I researched, reflected on, and re-imagined this collection of tales. I wondered how they would affect me, how our relationship would change.

I discovered that immersing myself in these elegantly simple stories was, indeed, potent medicine. Their clear-cut messages and vivid images stayed with me for weeks at a time. I found myself chanting little phrases from the tales and commentaries that helped me to be more accepting, to be more patient, to walk away from disagreements earlier and with greater ease. I felt wickedly wise when I noticed myself choosing silence at the right moments. (I was very pleased when I *recognized* the right moments.) I also stood firm at times when I was certain we needed to head off in a new direction. And whenever I looked at us as just another couple of sillies, it was hard to stay upset for too long.

This project also served as a celebration, a rousing affirmation of the years of diligent effort we've put into our marriage. Repeatedly, I saw aspects of our past behavior in the couples, but the shoes no longer fit. As we've mastered some tasks and new ones have arisen, our capacity for change and faith in our union have served us well; we can depend on our own best selves and each other to meet the next challenges. I have also felt our intention to serve our community grow and our commitment to one another deepen.

   May these stories be a blessing to you as they have blessed me in my marriage.

SOME THOUGHTS
FOR STORYTELLERS
ON USING THIS BOOK

> In a time lacking in truth and certainty
> and filled with anguish and despair, no
> woman should be shamefaced in attempt-
> ing to give back to the world, through her
> work, a portion of its lost heart.
>
> —LOUISE BOGAN

Twelve years ago I decided to present a storytelling concert celebrating marriage and partnership. It seemed like such a simple, straightforward task . . . but as I searched, I discovered that suitable stories for the show were actually quite elusive. Oh sure, there were many folk and fairy tales that ended with the joyful assurance that the hero and heroine lived "happily ever after." However, very few peeked behind that couple's door three, or thirteen, or thirty years later to observe the state of their union.

Most of the folktales that I found about married life fell into one of two categories: "humorous" stories that ridiculed the husband, or "humorous" stories that belittled the wife. That was not what I was looking for, not at all! So I searched contemporary short fiction, thinking that depictions of modern couples might be more evenhanded. What a shock! I found collection after collection of "love stories" so full of bitterness, cynicism, and despair that I felt like washing my hands after reading them to avoid contaminating my own relationship.

When I told people that I was having a hard time finding folktales about good marriages, their reply was, "Well, of course. A 'good marriage' story would be boring. There would be no conflict." I would just smile and change the subject. Inwardly I was thinking, *What do you mean, no conflict? Come around to my house some night when we're packing for a trip, or the afternoon before a big party. Hah!*

In Eastern European Jewish folk wisdom there is a saying: "You get married not because you never fight, but because you know how to make up." I wanted to find stories about people who were smart enough to know there would be fights but who got together anyhow. And I wanted to find the stories that would tell us how to make up.

You see, despite past experiences, grim statistics, and a barrage of distorted images from the media, people continue to get together. *A satisfying marriage is still rated as our number one goal*—ahead of wealth, health and success!* Since our communities value committed relationships so strongly, I wanted to create storytelling programs that would validate those heartfelt desires. While I think that storytelling can play a part in healing struggling relationships, I believe that it is most effective as part of a holistic approach to commitment, creating an atmosphere that supports success from the outset. Whenever I present stories that offer positive role models, encouraging messages, and realistic portrayals of problem solving, I know that I am making a contribution to the well-being of my community.

The institution of marriage has undergone radical change over the centuries, and its eminent demise has been predicted regularly during that time as well. Yet marriage has endured. However, a truly profound shift has occurred in the way we approach commitment, and it has happened *within our lifetime.* It is now possible for people to marry solely for their personal happiness and to legally divorce if they do not attain the happiness they expect. I believe that this current attitude reveals the underlying problem—not with the concept of couplehood itself, but with our crippling inability to create and sustain healthy relationships.

---

* Sollee, Diane, MSW , "Shifting Gears: An Optimistic View of the Future of Marriage," from Smart Marriages website (http://www.smartmarriages.com/optimistic.html), 1996.

Scores of books have been written about the history of marriage and the breakdown of marriage—individually and collectively. They tell how to fix your broken marriage or how to repair your life after your marriage fails. They are written by liberals, conservatives, Christians, New Age teachers, marriage therapists, lesbian scholars, and research scientists. They attribute the troubled state of marriage to lack of time, lack of money, lack of federally funded programs, too many federally funded programs, an absence of spiritual faith, patriarchy, abnegation of personal responsibility, no-fault divorce laws, cohabitation, popular culture, and inevitability.

Until recently, there has been little guidance available for developing satisfying unions. While plumbers, doctors, and beauticians must study intensively to be licensed for their work, virtually any couple can obtain a license to get married without any preparation. There is no "official couples training course," no job description offered, no social expectation that we should do anything to ready ourselves for the most significant commitment of our lives—except plan a wedding!

Nowadays there are many, many books, seminars, and workshops about creating good marriages, nurturing lasting relationships, and learning how to live with another human being (who, if you believe all that you read, may actually be from another planet). They say that getting to "happily ever after" is possible if you master nine developmental tasks, stay in touch with your inner feminine or deep masculine, learn how to "dialogue" about everything, practice "fair fighting," invite Jesus into the marriage, stop whining, and hold out for your soulmate.

While these books and trainings offer much valuable information and advice, I believe we need more than statistics and one-on-one exercises and professional opinions to change our beliefs about commitment and its consequences. *Transforming the way relationship is represented in our popular culture is crucial.* The stuff of our everyday lives— our music, television programs, magazine advertising, newspaper articles, movies and plays, novels, religious beliefs, Internet websites, American traditions, and folklore— impacts the way we perceive commitment and marriage tremendously. We are enmeshed in this mass of influences, both subtle and blatant. Sadly, in all of these areas, teenagers, young adults, and unhappy couples will find few positive stories to inspire and inform them. How can any couple create a successful bond if they live in our "culture of divorce," if they are inundated with images of couplehood as a source of endless romance and/or sexual gratification on demand, if they've never observed or experienced a solid, working relationship?

If you become interested in telling stories about successful partnership, I would suggest reading about marriage and relationships, both the good and the bad. It's important to know the issues your audiences are grappling with (or should be grappling with!) when structuring your program. You'll want to familiarize yourself with an assortment of material for various listeners. A classroom of high school students will benefit from a different set of stories than an audience of older, married adults.

Personally, I prefer tales with the characteristics of a companionate relationship, since these stories most accurately reflect the sea change of modern couplehood. This is the type of relationship that many of us in our thirties, forties, and early fifties are trying to negotiate. It has been labeled the most difficult style of marriage to establish and sustain because almost every facet of the relationship is being reinvented. You can read about "companionate marriage" in *The Good Marriage* (see Bibliography and Resources section). There are no traditional tales about companionate marriage per se, since it has only evolved in the last twenty-five years or so. Consider yourself lucky whenever you find a story that features a couple who shares responsibilities, respects one another as individuals and/or likes each other as friends.

There are several reasons why you won't find an abundance of "good marriage" folktales, most of them better suited to discussion in a folklore, psychology, or anthropology text. I think it is sufficient to say that it's challenging to find tales of egalitarian relationships in hierarchical societies—and the patriarchies of every major culture on Earth have been hierarchical in nature. The types of relationships we are now exploring have few historical precedents, in literature or in life. You won't read many examples of companionate marriage or gay civil union in the Brothers Grimm or a collection of Japanese folktales.

In the "high and far off times" when the oral tradition was an integral part of everyday life worldwide, marriage more often resembled a business partnership rather than a love match. Commoners looked for partners who were physically strong, fertile, and capable of managing farms, trades, or households. Merchants and nobility sought alliances that would consolidate power, property, and community. Romantic love was often hoped for and sometimes found, but it was not essential when considering prospective husbands and wives. Consequently, the folktales were products of their times. They were wry reflections from pragmatic men and women who too often had to make do with imperfect mates in order to survive.

That said, there is still plenty of material out there. Obviously, this is not a compilation of every "couple's story" I could lay hands on. No, I had some very specific considerations in mind as I sifted through hundreds upon hundreds of folktales to find the ones I wanted to include. There are tasks that each successful couple masters as they grow together, and there are serious dangers that each couple must avoid. There are qualities that men and women must bring to a partnership in order for it to thrive, and then there are some traits that have no place in a supportive relationship. These thoughts and others all influenced my decisions. And, of course, there was no guarantee that I would *find* a suitable tale simply because I *wanted* one to illustrate a certain principle.

Every teller has her own beliefs, her own messages, that she considers of primary importance. Chances are that you will find some gaps in this book that you'll want to fill with your own discoveries. The listing of sources mentions a number of other stories of merit that were not included, and the bibliography includes several collections that I found to be very comprehensive.

Once you've gathered a juicy batch of material to craft into a concert, you'll want to vary your program choices in terms of length, style, and tone. A good romance like "Sir Gawain and the Loathly Lady," a hearty laugh like "The Husband Who was to Mind the House," something poignant like "The Tiger's Whisker"—these make a nice mix . . . Avoid stringing together a group of stories that all hit the same note; select tales with a variety of themes, and don't be afraid to use the cautionary tales, the ones that inform through negative example. It's important, however, to make clear your intentions for telling those stories so that your listeners understand that you are not deliberately perpetuating stereotypes. That can be done in your introductory remarks and/or in your delivery of the story. Referring to the three categories of this book will help you design an effective, artistically balanced program.

A note of caution: please consider your motives for telling relationship stories; they will have a bearing on the stories you choose and how you present them. You don't have to be in an ideal partnership in order to tell effective stories about couples. Indeed, some of our most powerful stories will come from men and women who have been wounded in love. But you do need to be aware of your assumptions and biases, your doubts and fears. With proper perspective, your experiences can enhance and deepen your work. You can then present the toughest tales with dignity and respect for yourself and others. As a professional artist, it is your responsibility to seek guidance in crafting such stories for public performance.

I believe that storytellers serve their societies by acting as vision carriers. We create programs of nurturing, inspiring, thought-provoking stories that show us how to live in the world, and then we hold these visions for our communities. These images of possibility draw people along their paths toward personal fulfillment and social commitment. Imagine the long-term impact in your community if you incorporated three stories into your repertoire that celebrated commitment and offered ways to enrich relationships! Imagine taking them into family life classes in high schools and colleges, into churches and prisons, performing for women's groups, men's groups, singles and couples groups, as well as your other venues. If a substantial number of the tellers in this country chose to do this, we *would* help to transform the image of "relationship" in our world. Let us use our voices and our stories to educate couples' hearts.

SOURCES FOR THE STORIES

As I began this project, I earnestly vowed to myself that I would not change a word of any tale just to suit my own agenda. Who was I kidding? It didn't take long for me to realize that that was a completely unrealistic approach to the book, and it had not been the guiding principle behind many of the collections I researched, either. After poring through hundreds of tales about couples, and with the experience of twenty-odd years of telling, listening, and crafting to draw on, I decided to be respectful but bold. You understand, from the outset, that I have a particular vision and the stories have been directed toward fulfilling that vision. Another author could take these same stories and refashion them into a collection of humorous tales, wisdom tales, women's tales, or saints' tales.

For every story, I used my primary sources and research as a springboard and then dove deep into my own imagination to create new retellings with a fresh perspective. In general, what was lacking from the stories was *context*. Since the original listeners knew the background—the time, place, setting, stock characters, prevalent social attitudes—all of that was deleted from the original narratives. I researched each culture for clues about the settings, the marriage and relationship practices, the food and clothes and details of everyday life, then incorporated those gleanings into my work. Always mindful of my own twenty-first century values and preferences, I tried diligently to remain faithful to the traditions of the time and place in the various stories. At the same time, I was stretching and informing and focusing the tales so that they would be accessible and entertaining to readers as well as listeners.

These stories have also been enhanced by the presence of genuine couples, some larger than life, but all true reflections of the way we interact on intimate terms with one another. In some tales the original characters had no names, in others the husband was named but not the wife. I wanted each of these women and men to have distinctive personalities, to have traits that people would recognize as their own. Generally, I wasn't much interested in telling you what they looked like or what they wore, but I did want you to find out how they felt and how they acted, reacted, and responded to situations in their relationships.

In compiling the collection, I revisited many stories that I had recoiled from in the past. I began to see the potential in some of them, the underlying messages that were obscured by tedious stereotyping and cruel gender bias. Those difficult tales became easier to work with when I tempered them generously with humor, inflating the stupidity or nasty tempers or jealousy to the height of the absurd.

I have tried to create a consistent tone for all of these stories so that they better illustrate the messages I want to share. I have not altered the basic plotline of any tale or shoehorned a couple with a problem into a tale about something else. If you read the versions of these stories that I cite below, you would recognize mine as valid retellings of these traditional folktales.

THE HUNDRED YEAR FRIENDSHIP:
STORIES OF SUCCESS

"What He Loved Best of All"

Jacobs, Joseph, ed. "A Pottle of Brains." *More English Fairy Tales.* New York: G.P. Putnam's Sons, 1922.

Pugh, Ellen. "Morgan and the Pot of Brains." *Tales from the Welsh Hills.* New York: Dodd, Mead, 1968.

There are many, many tales of clever wives and simple-minded husbands, but few where the foolish fellow is portrayed sympathetically. This one is Aarne-Thompson Tale Type 910G, Motif J.163.2.1 (Fool told to get a pottle of brains).

The classic tongue-in-cheek tale of a loving, good-humored wife is "Gudbrand on the Hillside" from Asbjornsen and Moe's famous collection, *Popular Tales from the Norse.* A husband is sent off to market with a valuable cow and "trades down" to nothing. When Gudbrand's neighbor hears of his exploits, the man is certain that Gudbrand's wife will be furious with him for squandering their wealth and they lay a wager regarding her reaction. But as Gudbrand's wife listens to her husband's account of the day's activities, she enthusiastically approves his every decision, and Gudbrand wins the bet. We all deserve such tolerance and affection.

I've done a fair amount of research on fools over the years (as well as some firsthand observation of my own behavior). Since much of our negative perception of the fool is grounded in what we value, I tried to portray Willy without belittling or sentimentalizing him so that he could be understood more clearly.

"The Weaver King, the Warrior Queen"

Khatchatrianz, I. and Orloff, N. W., trans. "Anait." *Armenian Folk Tales.* Philadelphia: Colonial House, 1946.

I was deeply impressed by this tale of companionate-style marriage when I read a Russian version from the Caucasus, "Anait," in Katherine Ragan's *Fearless Girls, Wise Women and Beloved Sisters,* but I sensed that the tale she used was riddled with Communist ideology. Sure enough, I found earlier versions that were much truer to its older Armenian roots.

There are a number of Jewish tales that feature the weaving ruler motif, such as "Money Comes and Money Goes but a Skill Stays with You Forever" in *Stories within Stories* by Penninah Schram. I also found variants in two of Frances Carpenter's collections. "The Shah Weaves a Rug" is a Persian tale from *The Elephant's Bathtub: Wonder Tales from the Far East.* In "The Village of the Pure Queen," from *Tales of a Korean Grandmother,* a warring general stops during his campaign in a small village and a lovely young woman offers the tired, thirsty stranger a bowl of water so clotted with willow leaves that he can only take tiny sips. He is impressed with her wisdom and later marries her and makes her the Pure Queen of the realm. Throughout her life he reveres her wisdom and consults her in matters of state.

Anait (or Anahita) was the mother goddess of the Armenians for centuries, presiding over the waters, stars, Fate, and fertility. She was skilled in battle as well, a fierce warrior who protected her lover and her people. (Monaghan, Patricia, ed. *The New Book of Goddesses and Heroines.* St. Paul, Minn.: Llewellyn Publications, 1997.)

I sought out the most traditional and mythic dimensions of this tale and incorporated them whenever it was appropriate.

"Wealth, Wisdom, Women"

Frankel, Ellen, ed. "Elijah and the Three Wishes." *Classic Tales: 4000 Years of Jewish Lore.* Northvale, N.J.: Jason Aronson, 1989.

Schram, Penninah, ed. "Elijah's Three Gifts." *Tales of Elijah the Prophet.* Northvale, N.J.: Jason Aronson, 1991.

Another Elijah tale, "Seven Years of Blessings," was helpful in creating my story. I found several versions of it in *A Portion in Paradise and Other Jewish Tales,* translated by H.M. Nahmad. This is an outstanding story of partnership, a companion piece to "The Three Brothers"; in each version of the tale a worthy wife's charity, piety, and wisdom are present. Elijah appears to a wealthy man fallen on hard times as he labors in a field. Offered seven years of blessings now or at the end of his life, the man consults with his wife and she tells him to take the blessings immediately. With their new-found prosperity they perform countless acts of charity, and when Elijah returns at the end of the seven years to reclaim the boon, the wife insists that they be allowed to keep the blessings unless a more generous couple can be found. They remain prosperous to the end of their days.

I liked all of these tales because they stressed that the couples helped their community. I tried to include some specific examples of Leah's kindness and goodness.

This is AT Tale Type 750D, Three brothers each granted a wish by an angel visitor.

"One Hundred Coins"

Gernant, Karen, ed. and trans. "Axiu Cleverly Reads a Strange Letter." *Imagining Women: Fujian Folktales.* New York: Interlink Books, 1995.

Here is a tale about a companionate-style marriage from a culture we don't often associate with gender equality. Gernant points out that there was often a wide gulf between the idealized Confucian mores of the Chinese intelligentsia and the actual beliefs and customs of the common folk. Because of the pictorial nature of their system of writing, encoding messages in picture "letters" is a common motif in Chinese folklore. Adapted with permission of the author.

"The Linden and the Oak"

Bulfinch, Thomas, ed. "Baucis and Philemon." *The Age of Fable.* New York: Fawcett Publications, 1965.

Hamilton, Edith, ed. "Baucis and Philemon." *Mythology.* New York: Penguin Books, 1969.

I still remember reading this story in elementary school when we studied Greek and Roman mythology. It was in Sally Benson's *Stories of the Gods and Heroes,* with Steele Savage's pen-and-ink illustrations providing my first, enduring images of the ancient characters. Edith Hamilton claims that Ovid's *Metamorphosis* is the original source for this tale. Her version is an update of Bulfinch's florid nineteenth century prose.

I chose to retell this story from the old couple's perspective.

Philemon's beekeeping and Baucis's herb gardening are my touches, as well. After learning of the great reverence for the linden tree by the women of many early European cultures, I emphasized its presence in the story.

This is the first of several stories in the collection that feature a disguised immortal appearing before mortals and granting them gifts, blessings, or wishes. This one is AT Tale Type 750, Gods in Disguise Reward Hospitality.

BAD LUCK AND BIG TROUBLE: CAUTIONARY TALES

"When Peter Churned the Butter"

Pourrat, Henri. "The Husband Who was Never Pleased." *French Folktales.* New York: Pantheon Books, 1989.

Asbjornsen, Peter C. and Jorgen Moe. Trans. George W. Dasent. "The Husband Who was to Mind the House." *Popular Tales from the Norse.* Detroit: Grand River Books, 1971.

This rollicking tale has romped over most of the world. In Wales it's "Cow on the Roof," found in Clarkson and Cross's *World Folktales,* and Katharine Briggs includes it as verses to an English school song in *A Dictionary of British Folk-Tales.* In Russia, it's known as "The Peasant Who Did His Wife's Work," found in Afanasyev's *Russian Secret Tales.* It is AT Tale Type 1408, The Man Who Did his Wife's Work.

There's also a Nigerian tale about a bumbling husband and his long suffering wife. Despite his nerve-wracking behavior that actually endangers his family, the two remain polite and loving with each other. It's "The Woman, Her Husband, Their Children and the Dodo" from *Fearless Girls, Wise Women and Beloved Sisters.*

"Reflections on a Marriage"

Bang, Molly. trans. Garrett Bang. "The Mirror." *Men From the Village Deep in the Mountains.* New York: Macmillan, 1973.

This was the first version I recall reading, probably eighteen years ago. It is a popular tale throughout Southeast Asia. "Simple Wang," in *Best-Loved Folktales of the World*, is a Chinese version. A Korean warrior is rewarded with a mirror in "The Tiger Hunter and the Mirror," from Frances Carpenter's *Tales of a Korean Grandmother.* It is AT Tale Type 1336A, Man does not Recognize his own Reflection.

"A Cake for Sholom and Sarah"

Ausubel, Nathan, ed. "The Affair of the Rolling Trunk." *A Treasury of Jewish Folklore.* New York: Crown Publishers, 1954.

Weinrich, Beatrice S., ed. Trans. Leonard Wolf. "The *Melamed's* Trunk." *Yiddish Folktales.* New York: Pantheon Books, 1988.

The variant in the Weinrich collection does not include the money-saving motif, rather it focuses on the quarrel and the trunk's trip into town. In both of these tales, the *melamed* and his wife survive their dispute.

"The Selkie Wife"

Yolen, Jane, ed. "The Seal's Skin." in *Favorite Folktales from around the World.* New York: Pantheon Books, 1986.

In 1895, Jeremiah Curtin collected an oral version of this tale, "Tom Moore and the Seal Woman," for his book *Tales of the Fairies and of the Ghost World: Collected from Oral Tradition in South-West Munster.* Thomas Keightly included "The Mermaid Wife" in *The Fairy Mythology.* Yet another version comes from the other side of the world—"The Porpoise Girl," from William Lessa's *Tales from Ulithi Atoll, a Comparative Study in Oceanic Folklore*. This haunting, ancient story is also found as a ballad, "Grey Selchie of Sule Skerrie." This story is "The Seal Woman," AT Tale Type ML4080. Its principal motif is B651.8, Marriage to seal in human form.

"Who Should Close the Door?"

Jagendorf, Moritz A., ed. "There Are Such People." *Noodlehead Stories From Around the World*. New York: Vanguard Press, 1957.

I remember this folktale from childhood, when my sister received a large, illustrated copy of it as a Christmas present. Since this story is common throughout the world, I think it is safe to assume that foolish couples are common worldwide as well. Versions can be found in France, China, Pakistan, England, Turkey, Italy, Palestine, and Korea. Known as "The Silence Wager," it is AT Tale Type 1351.

"The Wife Who Would Not Be Pleased"

Clarkson, Atelia and Gilbert Cross, eds. "The Pigheaded Wife." *World Folktales*. New York: Charles Scribner's Sons, 1980.

This is one of those tales that used to set my teeth on edge. It can be downright vicious—in one version, "The Old Woman Against the Stream," from *Norwegian Folk Tales*, the husband *drowns* his wife in a fit of anger! But its messages are too important to ignore, so I toned down the nastiness and turned up the humor.

I'm sorry to report that this is another extremely well-travelled folk tale. It is AT Tale Type 1365A, "The Obstinate Wife." A variant from New Mexico, "The Headstrong Woman," found in *Cuentos: Tales From the Hispanic Southwest* by Jose Maestas, goes right to the heart of the matter. The entire tale concerns the couple crossing a raging river and the wife's fatal insistence on riding a spirited, unruly horse. There is a very similar Tale Type, 1365B, Knife or Scissors, featuring the same couple having an argument about cutting something. Unfortunately, they are near a body of water . . .

If you're looking for a tale about a stubborn *husband*, a wryly funny, fascinating one is "Uteritsoq and the Duckbill Dolls." It's found in *The Girl Who Dreamed Only Geese and Other Tales of the Far North* by Howard Norman.

THE HOPE CHEST: STORIES OF COMFORT AND GUIDANCE

"The Love Potion"

Courlander, Harold, ed. "The Tiger's Whisker." *The Tiger's Whisker and Other Tales and Legends from Asia and the Pacific.* New York: Harcourt, Brace and Company, 1959.

There is a well-known Ethiopian variant of this tale about a stepmother trying to win the heart of her stepson called "The Lion's Whiskers" in *The Lion's Whiskers: Tales of High Africa,* by Russell Davis and Brent Ashabranner. In keeping with Korean shamanic tradition, I made the sage a woman.

"The Sweetest Thing in the World"

Fillmore, Parker, ed. "Clever Manka." *The Shepherd's Nosegay.* New York: Harcourt, Brace and Company, 1950.

This beloved folktale is found all over Europe. It is AT Tale Type 875, The Clever Peasant Girl. Frances Carpenter included a saucy Chilean version, "Clever Carmelita," in *South American Wonder Tales*. "The Wife's One Wish," from *A Harvest of World Folktales,* is a Jewish variant that focuses only on a barren wife's clever ploy to save her marriage. At a pre-divorce feast ordained by their rabbi, her husband tells her that she may take whatever she likes best from their home. When he awakens from a drunken stupor at his father-in-law's, he is so touched by her devotion that they reconcile.

By far the cleverest women of all are the legendary wives of Weinsberg. The Grimms recorded their story as legend #493, which tells of King Conrad III's defeat of the Duke of Welf in 1140 and his subsequent siege of the castle of Weinsberg. The womenfolk of the town brokered the surrender terms; they would be allowed to leave with whatever they could carry in their arms. Imagine the shocked reaction when the gates of the castle opened and each woman came staggering out, *bearing her husband.* The king, reportedly amused and impressed, remained true to his word and allowed the men to leave unharmed.

"Who Knows What Could Happen?"

Jamali, Sarah P. "The Sign of the Tassel." *Folktales from the City of the Golden Domes.* Beirut: Khayats Booksellers and Publishers, 1965.

Ms. Jamali collected most of her tales from her mother-in-law while she was living in Iraq. It was refreshing to "hear" the distinctive voice of a storyteller in her version of this tale and the others in the book.

An oral source, Hassan Momenzadeh, says that this tale was as common in southern Iran as "Cinderella" is here.

"Strawberries"

Ross, Gayle. "Strawberries." *Homespun: Tales from America's Favorite Storytellers.* Ed. Jimmy Neil Smith. New York: Crown Publishers, Inc., 1988.

This story is reprinted by permission of the author, Gayle Ross. Ms. Ross is a direct descendant of John Ross, who was the chief of the Cherokee Nation during the Trail of Tears. She found this legend in James Mooney's *Myths of the Cherokees and Sacred Formulas of the Cherokees.*

"Keep Your Wife Well Fed"

Knappert, Jan. "Tongue Meat." *Myths and Legends of the Swahili.* London: Heinemann Educational Books, 1970.

The Swahili tribe of East Africa has had contact with Middle Eastern culture for well over a thousand years. The very name *Swahili* is an Arabic word for "people of the coast," hence, the Arabian influence on this tale is extensive. Jan Knappert travelled "up country" and along the coast from Mombasa to Dar-es-Salaam, collecting these tales from storytellers. Knappert's collected version served as the basis for my adaptation.

"Saint Peter's Blessings"

Bierhorst, John, ed. "St. Peter's Wishes." *Latin American Folktales.* New York: Pantheon Books, 2002. This tale was first collected in Cuba from a teller named Clemente Sarria, and appeared in Samuel Feijoo's collection, *Cuentos Populares Cubanos,* vol. 1 (Havana: Universidad Central de las Villas/Ucar Garcia, 1960).

Blecher, Lone T. and George Blecher, ed. and trans. "The Lazy Boy and the Industrious Girl. " *Swedish Folktales and Legends.* New York: Pantheon Books, 1993.

There are many folktales about divinities whose blessings or curses are questioned by their companions. Invariably divine wisdom prevails, as in this case, where St. Peter obviously knew what he was doing all along.

These stories combine AT Tale Type 759, Divine Acts are Vindicated, and AT Tale Type 822, Lazy Boy and Industrious Girl.

Our culture values literature and written communication highly, while our forms of entertainment have become increasingly visual. There is little room left for the long and leisurely, complex, image-rich oral story of the hearthside teller. But since people are still social creatures, stories remain, transmitted now as jokes or quick sketches over a meal with friends, mere shadows of their former selves. The stories this tale is based upon read like jokes, stripped down to skeletal remains with little detail or characterization and with moralistic "punchline" endings. There was not a word about the particular flaws of the "bad" husbands or how those good women addressed them, nor any hint of how the "bad" woman's husband handled her behavior in the original Hispanic tale. I passed them by the first time I read them, but later realized that with a little resuscitation, their message could be a real blessing.

"What Women Most Desire"

Hastings, Selina. *Sir Gawain and the Loathly Lady.* New York: Lothrop, Lee and Shepard Books, 1985.

This is one of my very favorite tales. I have heard it told by several fine tellers, most memorably Ed Stivender (his rendition is on his CD *Tellin' Time*). I have read many other versions, waded through both "The Wedding of Sir Gawain and Dame Ragnelle" and Chaucer's "Wife of Bath Tale" in Middle English verse, and have been telling it myself for close to twenty years. Heeding Alan Irvine's perceptive insight concerning this story (see "Why I Hate Lady Ragnell" in *Storytelling* magazine, Volume 13, Issue 1, 2001, pp. 20–21), I chose to reveal Arthur's answer to Gromer at the end of the tale.

The literary sources cited above are based on much older Celtic folktales related to the Kiss of Sovereignty. One such tale is "Niall of the Nine Hostages" from the Matthews' *Encyclopedia of Celtic Wisdom*. Recognizing the mythic elements of these folktales, I tried to convey a sense of the numinous, archetypal qualities of the characters.

ADDITIONAL RESOURCES

Here are a few resources to explore if you would like to enrich your relationship further. They could also be useful in developing stories and programs that celebrate couplehood.

RECOMMENDED BOOKS

Carter, Angela, ed. *The Old Wives Fairy Tale Book.* New York: Pantheon Books, 1990.

Eisler, Riane. *The Chalice and the Blade: Our History, Our Future.* San Francisco: Harper & Row, 1987.

Eisler, Riane and David Loye. *The Partnership Way.* San Francisco: HarperSanFrancisco, 1990.

Gottman, John, Ph.D. *Why Marriages Succeed or Fail.* New York: Simon & Schuster, 1994.

Larsen, Stephen and Robin. *The Fashioning of Angels: Partnership as Spiritual Practice.* West Chester, PA: Chrysalis Books, 2000.

McLaren, Nancy, ed. *The Art of Loving Well: A Character Education Curriculum for Today's Teenagers.* Boston: Boston University, 1998.

Ragan, Kathleen, ed. *Fearless Girls, Wise Women and Beloved Sisters.* New York: W.W. Norton & Co., Inc., 1998.

Wallerstein, Judith and Sandra Blakeslee. *The Good Marriage: How and Why Love Lasts.* New York: Warner Books, 1995.

Organizations

The Coalition for Marriage, Family & Couples Education
5310 Belt Road NW
Washington, DC 20015–1961
phone: 202–362–3332
website: www.smartmarriages.com
This is the best resource in the country for finding individuals, organizations, publications, centers, and conferences that promote couple enrichment and education.

Center for Partnership Studies
P.O. Box 30538
Tucson, AZ 85751
phone: 520–546–0176
website: www.partnershipway.org
This group supports gender reconciliation and the creation of widespread social change based on Riane Eisler's partnership model of relating. They offer information, workshops, and events.

The Loving Well Project
School of Education, Boston University
605 Commonwealth Avenue
Boston, MA 02215
phone: 617–353–4088
website: www.bu.edu/education/lovingwell
The Loving Well Project has developed a curriculum for adolescents about partnership and character education. They produced the anthology, *The Art of Loving Well.* For information or to order an anthology, contact Nancy McLaren at the address above.